M000033904

"I am glad to write brother, Dr. Clifford Self. He is a dear friend to me and my healing ministry. Ministering with him was a real inspiration. He is an anointed, giving, and creative man of God.

"The Holy Spirit has always been my mentor. His counsel puts you on the winning side of the cutting edge. Men who understand and have a real relationship with the Holy Spirit will experience uncommon wisdom and power for everyday living.

"The book you're holding in your hand just may 'click' in your spirit in the way your heart has desired. I treasure my copy."

—*Dr. Oral Roberts, Chancellor, Oral Roberts University*

"To me, the greatest need in the world today is responsible men. Certainly, that's God's desire and purpose for this phenomenon we call humanity. The trouble is, the blueprint for manhood is increasingly buried under 'world think,' false and misleading definitions and philosophies. My friend, Dr. Cliff Self, has dusted off the blueprint and presents it clearly and excitingly, illustrated by personal examples. If you're not a perfect man—you should read this book!"

—*Pat Boone, Award Winning Author, Entertainer, and Recording Artist*

"Women, this is the book you've wanted him to read—a masculine writing style that will entertain and empower your man to become God's man."

—*Lee Ezell, Best-selling Author*

"The Greek for submission speaks of accountability and *Man UP* addresses this important need in a man's life with insight and practicality, while providing the biblical and common-sense tools of how to bring our flesh under the submission of the Lordship of Christ. In doing so, *Man UP* provides the spiritual keys necessary for every man desiring that his life become a positive influence in a negative world. With concise teaching, Dr. Self goes a step further and positively shares with men how to become an honest leader in a world permeated with deceit, and a faithful husband in a world consumed with infidelity.

"*Man UP* has the potential to help every man move into his respective sphere of responsibility, with the clear understanding that any leadership or influence must flow from the rock-solid foundation of godly character."

—*Marcus D. Lamb President / Founder Daystar Television Network*

"When I first picked up the book *Man UP*, I thought it was geared to men only. I decided I would just browse through it to see how men think. But, as soon as I started reading the book it gripped my spirit, body, and soul in a way that I never would have imagined. Having just been betrayed by a number of friends, I was walking through the 'valley of the shadow of death' emotionally. I can tell you that reading this book set me free to forgive and move on to God's calling and destiny for my life! I e-mailed Dr. Cliff immediately to thank him and tell him what this book he had written for men did for this woman!"

—*Helen Pensanti M.D.*

"The fame of *Man UP* was so compelling that it travelled from the Protective Custody inmates (where I serve as Chaplain) to the other prison venues including the female inmates. We have about 9000 inmates and the deputies are glad for the popularity of *Man UP*. It brings a big smile to their faces.

—*Pastor Dick Paddock, Prison Chaplain*

"The book of your life has already been written. You are simply living out the movie version! With the Holy Spirit as your director,

Grace your editor—cutting and slicing the best of your actions—and with instructors like Dr. Cliff Self, you can become the leading star whose life will shine for all eternity. My friend, Dr. Cliff will help you stay in character as you Man UP for the role of your life. I admire and respect Dr. Cliff Self. I worked with him as a peer, pastoring in the same county. I have worked side by side with him as a part of our pastoral staff. His wisdom and wit gives him the edge needed to relate to men and the women in men's lives. With confidence and conviction I recommend you read this book."

—*Phil Munsey, Senior Pastor, The Life Church*

"*Man UP* will engage men to find God's favor in their lives and become Champions of Faith."

—*Peter Sumrall, LeSea Broadcasting*

"Dr. Self not only exposes the DNA of being the man but draws you into the path to manifest your God-given manhood."

—*Douglas Weiss, Ph.D., Executive Director of Heart to Heart Counseling Center, Author of "Get a Grip"*

"In this book Dr. Cliff Self lays out the formula for every man to rise above mediocrity and become a champion for God. Life presents many challenges to us as men and each of those challenges in and of themselves can derail a man's destiny. Dr. Cliff offers a fresh look at how to deal with these challenges, overcome them, and Man UP for God. It is a must read for every man who desires to change for the best."

—*Dr. Jim Willoughby, Senior Pastor, Echos of Faith*

"Talk about 'being catapulted into a whole new level of living!' In Dr. Cliff Self's new book, *Man UP*, that's exactly what will happen to every man with an open heart to the work of the Holy Spirit! Explosive, insightful, compelling, and captivating—*Man UP* will clarify, focus, and ignite every man's life with a fresh perspective and real answers so desperately needed in today's world. Thank you, Dr. Self, for your uncompromising commitment to tackle a topic that will make a difference in our generation, where many people have lost their sense of direction but are in pursuit of real solutions!"

—*Dr. Art Sepúlveda, Word of Life Christian Center,*
Honolulu, HI, Author of Focus *and* Dream by Design

"Dr. Cliff Self has a unique way of communicating the truth of how to live life so that it pleases God and makes a man successful in business and home. It's all based upon relationships with God and man. When a person has his relational priorities in order, he cannot be anything but successful. I highly recommend the reading and studying of this book. It will help you to order your life aright so that you can live in peace and experience true happiness."

—*Ron Halvorson, President, Bethel Christian College*

"*Man UP* leads the reader into understanding the greatest secret in the universe: who is the Holy Spirit and how does He help you choose the right course of action every time. This is a must read for all who want to experience God and not just know about God."

—*Paul Long, Pastor, Solid Rock Church*

"Dr. Self has written a book that will bring out the real man in every man. This is a book for those that want to put away childish things. If you're serious about change, get this book. If you are comfortable where you are, buy a sports magazine."

—*Dr. Orlando Barela, Household of Faith Family Church*

Release the Champion in You!

Dr. Cliff Self

Mobile, AL

Man UP
by Dr. Cliff Self
Copyright © 2009 Dr. Cliff Self

All rights reserved. This book is protected under the copyright laws of the United States of America. This book may not be copied or reprinted for commercial gain or profit. Unless otherwise identified, Scripture quotations are taken from the New King James Version of the Bible, © 1982, Thomas Nelson, Inc. Scripture marked NLV is taken from the New Living Translation, ©1996, Tyndale Charitable Trust. Scripture quotations marked NLT are taken from the Holy Bible, New Living Translation, ©1996. Used by permission of Tyndale House Publishers, Wheaton, Illinois 60189. Scripture marked AMP is taken from the Amplified Bible (AMP), The Zondervan corporation, ©1987 by the Lockman Foundation. All rights reserved.

ISBN 978-1-58169-313-3
For Worldwide Distribution
Printed in the U.S.A.

Evergreen Press
P.O. Box 191540 • Mobile, AL 36619
800-367-8203

Dedication

I want to dedicate this book to all the strong men who have searched for a better way and did not give up. I salute you for the effort it takes to be the man you are. You have stepped out to find out that when you hook up with the Holy Spirit, you will discover purpose and fulfillment in life. You will be empowered to release the champion in you! I commend you for deciding to Man UP and become the champion God created you to be.

Table of Contents

Acknowledgments

There are so many people who played a part in making this book a reality. I have been blessed with so many wonderful people who have made such an impact on my life.

I want to acknowledge my mentors. Throughout my life, I have had many mentors who did not know they were my mentors. Their lives, ministries, and teachings have touched my life and birthed necessary changes for successful living. T.D. Jakes and Mike Murdock have been mentors through their teaching ministries. John Osteen made a tremendous impact on my life in the early years of my ministry. Dr. Oral Roberts has exemplified integrity and wisdom for which all men should strive. His friendship and assistance in writing this book are cherished memories.

Dr. Ed Cole was a true mentor. He took me into his confidence and taught me as his "young Timothy." His legacy still ministers to men around the world.

Known by the names Mr. White Bucks, Mr. Clean, Mr. America, and many other endearing names, Pat Boone has proven that in the entertainment world it is possible to Man UP and live by sound principles that produce a legacy. I want to say thank you to Pat for his assistance and encouragement in writing this book.

Thank you to Matt Crouch for his prayers and encouragement as a friend.

To my children, Scott and Christina, whom I love, each in unique and unexplainable ways. I have enjoyed serving you as Dad. You continue to bring me joy as you discover the principles of righteousness and purposeful living. Thank you for allowing me to share freely our story of love and discoveries together. I want to acknowledge my son-in-law, Perry. His loving faithfulness to my daughter and grandchildren is true evidence that he knows how to Man UP for all situations that a husband and father must endure.

Liz Cruz and Richard Finch are appreciated for their friendship and untiring help for their tenacious assistance with editing and creative ideas.

I want to thank my publishers for their professionalism and dedication to excellence. Their help in arranging the message of *Man UP* is greatly appreciated. God bless Evergreen Press.

To my wife, Darlene, the most winsome woman in the world and love of my life: We have weathered fierce storms together, and I realize how strong yet soft you are. Becoming a man has been for the most part a pleasurable journey. This is due largely to Darlene, the wise and wonderful woman in my life. Her beauty and charm have taught me grace. Her smile and patience have taught me wisdom. Her skill as a mother has taught me joy. Her diplomacy has earned me favor in the marketplace. I am blessed among men with the gift from God of my wife. I would not want to make this journey without her. Thank you, dear, for being more than wonderful. You are a distinctive woman, and I am wild about you!

Foreword

Have you ever been intrigued by one of those men who has a secret smile? Dr. Cliff Self is one of those rare men who still giggles and chuckles with a dimpled grin. He relishes life as a banquet and attacks it with a king-sized fork, knife, and lobster bib. His insatiable appetite is contagious.

What is he hungry for? He's hungry for men to be raised up with a passion for intimacy with the Holy Spirit, and for every man in his "hood" to realize he has a date with destiny and purpose. His clarion call provokes a divine awakening that celebrates the fullness of the intrinsic God potential.

He joyously beckons all men to discover and relish their identity. And wonder of wonders, he places tools in their hands to ultimately grasp the realization of their supernatural connection. In other words, men are uniquely created to be courageous champions!

We often tease that one of the names for the Holy Spirit is "Holy Sneaky." Through the fast paced and often humorous writings of our friend, Dr. Cliff Self, you will experience the reality of "A spoon full of sugar helps the medicine go down." Before you know what has happened, the Holy Spirit will have snuck into your heart, and you will be forever changed. Perhaps, you'll learn a secret or two that will cause others to question your smile.

Pastors Dony and Reba Rambo-McGuire
Grammy Award winners, The River at Music City

Introduction

Each year from December 26th through the first week of January, the College Bowl Championship series presents the best colleges in America competing for the National Championship Football title. It is an exciting week for football fans.

While watching the multitude of games this year, I kept hearing a common term being used by the various teams and coaches. The term was *power up*. They were communicating that it was time to put everything aside except for what pertained to the football game and draw upon all that was in each team member to compete and win the championship. I like the picture the term "power up" leaves in my mind. So while ministering to men around the country, I have been using the term *Man UP*.

To Man UP means to be all the man I was created to be. **When I Man UP, I tap into all the power of manhood. I release the champion in me and accomplish supernatural results.** How did I get to be a man? Do I qualify as a real man, or do I fall short? How do you Man UP and get the power and wisdom needed for manhood? How do you handle life as a real man? We must make the Man UP discovery.

Dr. Lloyd Ogilvie, who served as Chaplain to the United States Senate, tells the story of Senator Max Cleland from Georgia. Senator Cleland lost both legs and his right hand when a grenade accidentally exploded on a hilltop in Vietnam. He spent many years haunted by fearsome memories from the accident and fearful thoughts about making it through life.

Senator Cleland was twenty-five years old when in an

effort to rescue 5,000 marines who were surrounded by more than 20,000 North Vietnamese, Captain Max Cleland jumped off the helicopter, followed by the men under his command. Max noticed a grenade on the ground; thinking it was his, he went toward it. The grenade exploded. His eyeballs were jammed into his skull. His ears rang with deafening vibrations. When the smoke cleared, his right hand and most of his right leg were gone, and his left leg was a smoldering mass of bloody flesh. Senator Cleland lived for years with the agony that this tragedy was his own fault.

After Senator Cleland shared his story on a television talk show, David Lloyd, a former marine who had served on that hill in Vietnam, who had seen the show, called Senator Cleland. He told the Senator that after the explosion, he wrapped a tourniquet around Max's thigh. Then he tended to another soldier covered with blood. This was the young man's first day in combat. He cried out to Lloyd, "It was my grenade! It was my grenade!" Out of inexperience, the soldier had loosened the pins on his grenades to make them easier to activate in combat and then dropped one of them. It had not been Max's grenade. Hearing this revelation removed the self recrimination that had plagued the Senator for over thirty-one years.

You are about to Man UP and make the discoveries that will change you forever. As you read this book, you will discover that all the action, drama, and comedy of your life have already been scripted for you. While you are performing as the leading man in this play called life, each scene will mandate different qualities of manhood. You may be called upon to perform as a military man, a repairman, the rain man, a rebel, a political figure, or even as superman. Fear not.

You have a supernatural director who assists you and assures you of an award winning performance when you Man UP.

Even Jesus had to discover how to Man UP (Luke 2:52). When faced with great stress while having to make life changing decisions, Jesus would Man UP and receive the encouragement, direction, and empowerment for accomplishing supernatural results (Matthew 26:37-39). If Jesus, the great I AM, had to Man UP, surely we need to discover this secret.

WOW! It happened to me. I discovered how to Man UP in the summer of 1986. My life was dramatically changed. I met the Holy Spirit as a person. I discovered that God creates unforgettable encounters with Himself. These encounters are to give us the ability to Man UP.

My mother died when she was fifty-two. When I was that age, I was given thirty days to live. It was time to Man UP. Before learning to Man UP, my father was married five times to three different women. My nephew married as a young man in his 20s, eager to be a father. His wife has experienced several miscarriages. He had to discover how to Man UP and help his wife to recover. My father-in-law was happily remarried for five years when his bride died of cancer. You can't survive these types of life experiences without knowing how to Man UP. I think you will agree, as you discover how to Man UP, release the champion in you, and accomplish supernatural results, you will have uncovered the greatest secret of manhood—the ability to Man UP.

Prepare to have an encounter that will change you forever. Prepare to get the answers and the power for real manhood as you discover purpose and fulfillment in life. Man UP! You will enjoy the journey.

Chapter 1

The Man UP Mandate

I have always wanted to be a champion. I never wanted to be average or mediocre. Even as a boy, I dreamed about doing great things in the world. One day I decided to try and make my baby brother, Chuckie, into a champion. That was a potentially fatal mistake! Chuckie asked me to fix his breakfast. Now Chuckie was one of those kids who would usually eat anything, but this morning he wanted cereal for breakfast. We only had generic wheat flakes in the house, but I wanted to make him the breakfast of champions.

I poured him a bowl full of the ordinary wheat flakes, but they didn't "snap, crackle, and pop" like I thought a breakfast of champions should. Unfortunately I had gotten my cereals mixed up. I didn't know that wheat flakes could never be Rice Krispies with their popping noises, no matter what I did. I decided to find something to put into his cereal to rev it up. I searched under the sink and found Drano (a powerfully corrosive chemical household drain cleaner) and put it on his cereal. I was sure it would make his cereal get explosive, but I did not know it was full of poison. I told Chuckie to look at how pretty and sparkly and bubbly his cereal had become. I told him it was the breakfast of champions, so to eat it up, and he began to do just that. Of course I knew that the substance was not sugar, but I had no idea what it was or that it could kill him.

A few minutes later, he was gagging on the cereal and screaming bloody murder. I had enough sense to run into my parents' bedroom and wake them up. When I told them what I had done, they rushed Chuckie to the hospital and pumped out his stomach. Thankfully he lived. When my parents came home, they applied the "board of education" to my "seat of knowledge," and I learned that Drano is not an appropriate ingredient for breakfast cereals.

My brother ate the stuff because he wanted to be a champion. He didn't know it was bad for him. He thought it would taste like sugar, and it looked great. He put his confidence in his big brother, and it almost killed him. He didn't read the label himself; he didn't even know how to read, and I certainly didn't try to find out any information about it. He ate that cereal, thinking it was going to make him a champion; instead, it was designed to destroy him!

The above story sadly describes the status of many men today. We have ingested something we think is good for our manhood, and it's killing us. We've heard so many ideologies about manhood that it can be confusing. We have learned how inadequate we are as men and how fierce the devil is. What we have not focused on is how big our God is and what intimacy with the Holy Spirit can do for our manhood. *"Greater is He who is in us than he who is in the world"* (1 John 4:4); *"I can do all things through Christ who strengthens me"*

(Philippians 4:13). We have not discovered the secret of how to truly Man UP.

Intimacy with the Holy Spirit releases the wisdom and power we need for anything we will ever face as men. Before we discuss intimacy, though, let's discuss courage. It takes courage to enable a man to experience intimacy.

Courage is a vital ingredient that has been missing from the lives of too many men. If we have courage, we shall have victory in all things! If we ingest anything else, if we put our confidence in anyone other than God and His promise that He is with us, it will poison us; and we'll need to get our spiritual stomachs pumped!

Courage is what enables us to face danger with confidence. It is what helps us to take healthy risks and not foolhardy ones for the benefit of others as well as ourselves. The key to having courage is to know that God is indeed with us no matter whom or what we face, and we need to release His greatness and direction into our circumstances.

God's Direction

A mandate is an official order or direction to do something. It also contains the authority to carry out that course of action. As we will see, God has given men the mandate to Man UP and arise above foolishness or even mediocrity to greatness. This mandate demands courage for it to be accomplished. This courageous mandate is a command found in Joshua 1:6-9 where God states the mandate to Man UP.

Be strong and of good courage, for to this people you shall divide as an inheritance the land which I swore to their fathers to give them. Only be strong and very courageous, that you may observe to do according to all the law which Moses My servant commanded you; do not turn from it to the right hand nor to the left, that you may prosper wherever you go. This Book of the Law shall not depart from your mouth, but you shall meditate in it day and night, that you may observe to do all that is written in it; for then you will make your way prosperous, and then you will have good success. **Have I not commanded you? Be strong and of good courage;** *do not be afraid, nor be dismayed, for the Lord your God is with you wherever you go* (emphasis added).

We have been instructed to take courage from God. Courage is the knowledge that God is with us wherever we go. That knowledge will equip us to fight for our wives, sons, daughters, and possessions. God sent Jesus to die for us so we could live life more abundantly (John 10:10). Satan wants to stop the benefits of that abundant life. When he lashes out at us, we begin to wonder, "Where is God? Why does He allow rotten things to happen?" Many times we blame God for our problems! But in reality, it is Satan who wants to make God miserable, and he strikes at God through His people.

If we let this happen, it is because we don't take courage from God and stand firm on the knowledge that God is with us wherever we go. As men, if we don't know how to fight for our families and homes, we will lose them. If we don't know how to take courage from God, all that we cherish will be gone because we have a fierce enemy who is a thief and a destroyer.

Imprint God on Your Minds

The prophet Nehemiah tells us *"Do not be afraid of the enemy;* [earnestly] *remember the Lord and **imprint Him** [on your minds], great and terrible; and* [take courage from Him] *to fight for your brethren, your sons, your daughters, your wives, and your homes'"* (Nehemiah 4:14 AMP, emphasis added).

A popular example of imprinting is the duckling. Whatever the duck first sees when it is hatched, it believes to be its mother. I had a pet duck when I was young, and that little thing really thought I was its mother! I would take it out of the box and when I walked down the street, the duck would follow me, quacking all the way to the end of the block and back again. That duck had imprinted on its mind that I was "Mama."

In the above verse, Nehemiah tells us to imprint on our minds the great, the terrible, the awesome God. This is not a suggestion; he is mandating us to imprint God on our minds! As a result of seeing God as the all-powerful person He really is and knowing that He is with us, we will have all the courage we need.

What do we do with that supernatural courage? Fight! As men, it is necessary to fight. We must fight—against the old sin-nature, against the powers of darkness, against unbelief, and against Satan's onslaughts of sickness, poverty, and fear. But we must always take courage and remember that we have been given the promise of victory! *"Take the shield of faith, with which you will be able to quench all the fiery darts of the wicked one"* (Ephesians 6:16). *"Now thanks be to God who always leads us in triumph in Christ"* (2 Corinthians 2:14).

When I know God is with me, I can hold up the shield of

faith, which is His Word. I'll act on His Word, and that will quench all the fiery darts coming against me. If I don't know God is with me, I won't have the courage to act on His Word. If I don't know that God is with me, I won't be able to hold up the shield of faith.

How do we know for certain that He is with us? The same way we know anyone else is with us: by communication. This communication is called prayer. When we talk with God in prayer, we have fellowship with Him. When we spend time with Him, listen to Him and value His truth, we are sure of His presence in our lives, and this produces courage.

Prayer produces intimacy with the One to whom we pray. That's why the disciples begged Jesus to teach them how to pray. They understood the importance of fellowship and communication with God.

How should you pray? Just talk to God the same way you talk to anyone else. Increase your intimacy with God by sharing your thoughts and questions with Him. He will gladly receive your effort and not rebuke you (James 1:5). The Holy Spirit will then take your words and present them to God and begin to instruct you how to pray (Romans 8:26).

The devil's lying communication can keep us from prayer. He can yell so loud that it is sometimes easy to think, *God is mad at me. He doesn't love me because I haven't done everything He wanted me to do.* Satan throws our sins against us. But the Bible tells us that we have an advocate in Jesus Christ, who is faithful and cleanses us from all unrighteousness (1 John 2:1-2; 1:9).

Satan loves to distract us from the truth that God is with us by getting us to focus our attention on his lies. We can't let the enemy get us off track. Instead, we are to use our energy to overcome Satan, enabling us to stay focused and in communication with God. We can confidently raise our shield of faith with the courage that we've taken from knowing that God is with us.

Man UP and Arise to Greatness

The Man UP mandate tells us if we will take courage from God, we will rise to greatness! In speaking of His cousin, John the Baptist, Jesus said: *"Assuredly, I say to you, among those born of women there has not risen one greater than John the Baptist; but he who is least in the kingdom of heaven is greater than he"* (Matthew 11:11).

Notice that John was not born great—he rose to greatness. Among those born of women at the time of Jesus, there was none greater than John the Baptist. A goal of my life is to be one of those whom, like John the Baptist, Jesus calls "great"—not for my own sake, but for His, that His kingdom might be expanded. Jesus said that the least of us in His kingdom today could be greater than John the Baptist. WOW!

We are not born great. There is no such thing as the birth of a great preacher, a great prophet, a great king, a great lawyer, or a great doctor. There is no great anything ever born! Only baby boys and baby girls are born. Those babies will eventually arise to either greatness or mediocrity through their understanding of the process of greatness and choosing accordingly. God doesn't expect us to leave this world until the world knows we have been here. We are empowered for greatness when we Man UP and know God is with us.

The desire for greatness only becomes an improper motivation when we think of it in terms of comparing ourselves with someone else or when we do it for self gratification. But when we realize that God calls us to a life of greatness to serve Him and others, we have a pure motivation. Jesus tells us that it is good to seek greatness with certain provisions: *"Whoever therefore breaks one of the least of these commandments and teaches men so, he will be called least in the Kingdom of Heaven; but whoever does and teaches them, he will be called great in the Kingdom of Heaven"* (Matthew 5:19 NAS). I want to be called great in the kingdom of God. I am going to live so that even my enemies must call me great, because God calls me great in His kingdom!

God has called us to "life abundant," not "life mediocre." He says: *"I have come that you might have life, and that you may have it more abundantly"* (John 10:10). There is nothing mediocre about Jesus or the lifestyle He offers. Mediocrity is the curse of the ignorant—the devil's lie that we should not expect anything more.

We are destined for greatness. We are destined to win! It is God's mandate for men to Man UP by taking courage and rising to greatness. God tells us to take our courage from Him for the purpose of fighting for the inheritance that Jesus Christ has given to us. When we know how to Man UP and release the champion in us, we will accomplish supernatural results.

You have embarked on a journey to greatness. You will not settle for mediocrity when you accept the mandate from God to Man UP. This journey will demand courage and anointing from God.

In the next chapter, we will discuss specifically how to

take this courage from God and be anointed to arise to greatness. You are on the way to becoming the champion God created you to be!

Chapter 2

The Courageous Man

Have you ever been afraid to see yourself naked? Has seeing your spouse naked ever frightened you? Now that is a dangerous question! When Adam and Eve discovered they were naked, waves of fear shot through them. This reaction has been affecting men ever since that time.

When Adam forsook the Man UP mandate, he lost his courage. He lost sight of God being with him and focused on his own nakedness instead. This change of focus gave birth to fear. When Adam refused to Man UP after Eve offered him the fruit of the forbidden tree, fear was born on earth for the first time in history. Up until this time, man lived courageously in the presence of God and enjoyed supernatural results. When Adam refused to Man UP, he made his deal with the devil and was disqualified from experiencing the supernatural life he had been enjoying.

After Adam's choice not to Man UP, God came into the garden and called to Adam, "Where are you?" Adam answered, "I heard Your voice, and I was afraid because I was naked; and I hid myself" (Genesis 3:10).

He was afraid because he was naked! Fear is knowledge of our inadequacies (our nakedness). Weren't Adam and Eve naked before? Yes, but they didn't have knowledge of it because their former thoughts were solely centered on God. All they had considered was God—their Creator, the supernatural, almighty One who fashioned heaven and earth, and who walked with them and had fellowship with them. As a result they were crowned with God's glory. Now the glory had left them, and they knew they were naked. God inquired of them, "Who told you that you were naked?" They responded exactly as you and I sometimes do today: they blamed everybody else! Adam blamed Eve, and Eve blamed the serpent.

The refusal of Adam to take courage and Man UP to fight the serpent's cunning attack gave birth to fear. And so, Adam and Eve began to focus on their inabilities. **Fear is the awareness of our inabilities,** which takes away from us the knowledge that God is with us wherever we go.

Remember God's command in Joshua 1:9, "I command you to know that I am with you wherever you go, so don't be discouraged." In other words, do not concentrate on what you don't have or what you think you can't do. This is not an option—it is a command. It is the Man UP mandate!

Without a clear focus on the fact that God is with me, I will not be able to believe that there is any possibility for supernatural results. I was touched by a true story of courage told by Hal Lindsey. In a Communist country, the church had to hide from the eyes of officialdom. Christians would use elusive measures to keep from being discovered. However, many times the secret police would find them anyway, and then they would force various degrees of humiliation and punishment upon the believers. One night, a group of church members were clandestinely meeting in the basement of a home. While they were worshiping, the doors burst open and several KGB officers and soldiers entered, machine guns at the ready.

The Christians were harshly ordered to stand against the wall. The officer in charge barked, "If you will renounce this nonsense about Jesus Christ right now, we will let you go without harm." The majority of the church members immediately made their decision and left quickly. Several Christians remained undecided, and the ultimatum was repeated: "If you will just forget about this foolishness, we will let you go. Otherwise . . ." More believers departed.

Finally, only a few stalwarts remained—a father and his children, and a scant handful of others. The tense minutes dragged on as the Christians stared at machine guns pointed at their heads and read the menacing expressions on the faces of the KGB soldiers. At length, when no one else made a move to surrender their beliefs, the leader of the KGB said, "Now . . . raise your hands. We will praise the Lord together!" Astonishingly, this entire KGB troop, sent a week before to break up another such meeting, had instead accepted Jesus Christ as their Lord and Savior! The one thing they knew was that unless you are willing to die for what you believe, you cannot be trusted!

Can I be trusted as a man? Does God trust me to carry His presence and power into my everyday circumstances? Am I willing to Man UP and live courageously? For what am I willing to die? What is my true belief system? Do I focus on fear (my nakedness), or do I believe that God is with me to enable me to rise above mediocrity to greatness? To do this demands courageous living. Only the courageous can arise to greatness. We are called to Man UP and be great. The greater One lives in us as believers in Jesus Christ (1 John 4:4). Remember, to Man UP is to take courage and release the greatness that is within you.

Shark Bait or Lion Food?

Blood attracts sharks. When I lived in Florida, I remember one day when a seven hundred pound hammerhead shark was spotted off the pier. The shark was shot and killed with a rifle, and then it was hooked and pulled to shore. The water was cleared of people because the blood from the killed shark was attracting other sharks. Somehow, sharks can sense or smell blood—even from as far as a mile away—and they rush toward it. When blood hits the water, it spreads quickly. Fear is like blood hitting the water; it spreads quickly and attracts all the sharks of hell.

Satan uses fear to shift our concentration from the fact that God is with us—He is our Emmanuel—to get our focus on our own inadequacies and inabilities. God says we have mighty weapons to pull down strongholds and the power to cast down those imaginations:

Casting down arguments, and every high thing that exalts itself against the knowledge of God, bringing every thought into captivity to the obedience of Christ (2 Corinthians 10:5).

We are to courageously cast down anything that goes against the knowledge that He is with us. We need to follow the command to have courage so we can hold up the shield of faith and quench all the fiery darts of the enemy. If fear enters one area of our lives, it will defile others. For instance, fear over the circumstances in our jobs can affect our relationship with our children, our marriages, and our health.

Fear is also an illusion. The African lion uses fear to catch its prey. The lion goes to the watering hole and lies in wait in the tall grass for "dinner" to come to drink. When the antelopes, gazelles, or other prey come to the watering hole, they look around to see whether any enemies are there. They won't see the lion because he's hidden—camouflaged—from view. They decide that it's safe and go down to the water to drink. While they are drinking, the lion lets loose a mighty **"R-r-o-o-a-r-r-r!"** which echoes off the water. The herd freezes in fear because they can't see the hidden lion, and they can't tell where the sound is coming from. While the prey is trying to figure out what to do or where to go, the lion pounces and drags off his supper. *"Be sober, be vigilant; because your adversary the devil walks about like a roaring lion, seeking whom he may devour"* (1 Peter 5:8).

When Satan uses fear in our lives, we usually don't see him hiding. Even when we come to take a drink of living water (an awareness of God's presence), he stands up and roars that we are ugly, stupid, and sinful; he tries to get us to concentrate on ourselves instead of the knowledge that God is with us. If we listen to him instead of concentrating on God, he will just drag us down and consume us. But if we refuse that lie and don't try to argue, but rather cast away that imagination and throw out anything against the knowledge of the fact that God is with us, we will remain courageous! *"For God has not given us a spirit of fear; but of power, and of love, and of a sound mind"* (2 Timothy 1:7 KJV). God did not give us fear. He gave us power, love, and soundness of mind to make the right choices. So we need to Man UP, take courage from God, and fight. If we do, we will subdue all the devil's attacks against us.

Faith With Courage

We cannot hold up the shield of faith without courage. It takes courage to operate faith. Faith is a gift. Courage is a command. It is *not* an option. It is not a gift. It is a command. It is the Man UP mandate! (Joshua 1:9)

Courage is not the absence of fear; it is the mastery of fear. We can take courage from God. If we don't take courage from Him, we won't have it; and if we don't have courage, we will give into circumstances and fail. Paul said it this way:

> *Let us also lay aside every weight and the sin which so easily ensnares us, and let us run with endurance the race that is set before us, looking unto Jesus, the Author and Finisher of our faith, Who for the joy that was set before Him endured the cross, despising the shame, and has sat down at the right hand of the Throne of God* (Hebrews 12:1-2).

Paul is encouraging us to run the race with endurance—with patience, determination, and steadfastness—and to lay aside the weights *and the sin* (did you notice "sin" is singular not plural) by looking to Jesus, the Author and finisher of our faith.

Courage is comprised of the following five elements that are listed in Isaiah 43: creation, redemption, identification, possession, and protection.

But now, thus says the Lord...
1. ***Who created you,*** *O Jacob, and He Who formed you, O Israel, "Fear not, for*
2. ***I have redeemed you;***
3. ***I have called you by your name;***
4. ***You are Mine****! When you pass through the waters, I will be with you; and through the rivers, they will not overflow you. When you walk through the fire,*
5. ***You will not be burned,*** *nor shall the flame scorch you. For I am the Lord your God, the Holy One of Israel, your Savior"* (Isaiah 43:1-3 emphasis added).

1. Creation

God says in effect, "I created you. You are not an accident. You may have been a surprise to Mom and Dad, but you are not an accident." He scheduled your arrival on planet earth. He says He knew you before you were formed in your mothers' womb: *"Before I formed you in the womb, I knew you; and before you were born, I sanctified you"* (Jeremiah 1:5). Nothing Satan can say will alter this fact: God—who created us and has always known us—is always with us. Therefore, the first element in taking courage is to know that God Himself, the Almighty Lord of the universe, created us specifically as we are. In other words, we are the direct result of God's planning, His own creation.

2. Redemption

"I have redeemed you." That means that not only did He create us, but He also put a value on us. He paid a price for us. Lots of people clip coupons to save money and receive an amount off the retail price when they redeem their coupons

at the time of purchase. But God paid full price for us. He didn't shop around for the best bargain or haggle to get a discount for us. He paid top dollar. He spent His one and only beloved Son and heir, Jesus Christ, to buy us back from the kingdom of darkness:

> *For God so greatly loved and dearly prized the world that He (even) gave up His only-begotten (unique) Son, so that whoever believes in (trusts, clings to, relies on) Him shall not perish (come to destruction, be lost) but have eternal (everlasting) life* (John 3:16 AMP).

God thought enough of us to sacrifice His only begotten Son for us. He bought us back from the devil, so we mustn't allow anyone to tell us that we are unimportant or without value. And we should never tell God that He's a poor businessman because He paid too much for us! To take courage, we must know that God has redeemed us.

3. Identification

"I have called you by your name." We are not labeled "six-six-six." We are not a number to God—He has called us by name. He's the God of individuals, not a corporate God. He is our God. The Bible says that He knows the number of hairs on our head—even if that number changes hourly! That may seem trivial to us, but that's how intimate He desires to be. We are not lost in the crowd with God. Any ideas contrary to that knowledge need to be cast down and thrown away so we will Man UP and maintain courage.

4. Possession

"You are mine!" We are not our own, so we must quit

17

living as if we are. He owns us, He is God, and He can do what He wants, when He wants, unchallenged. The Bible says that what belongs to Him is holy. The Bible also says that He won't allow what is His to be plucked from His hands. He will fight for us and vindicate us. Any idea or thoughts contrary to that need to be cast down because they are against the knowledge of God's Word and character.

5. Protection

"You will not be burned." When we go through the fire, we can hold up the shield of faith and quench any flames that threaten to destroy us. We are going to come out of the fire, and we won't be scorched or even smell of smoke! When we Man UP and take courage through the fiery infernos we experience in life, everybody watching is going to say, "Whoa! Your God is *the* God!" Just as Nebuchadnezzar did with Shadrach, Meshach, and Abednego, the world will have to acknowledge that the all-powerful God is with us. Take the time to read the account in Daniel 3. It will motivate your manhood.

Let me go back a bit. The Bible said, "*When* you pass through the fire . . ." not "*If* you pass through the fire . . ." And notice that we pass *through* the fire, we don't stay there; we don't live there. There is a journey from point A to point B that we need to make. It is a place of passage. There is a completion date scheduled for our trip through the fire. We are not going to live there. When we go through the waters, God will be with us and will protect us, so we need to Man UP, take courage from God, and fight!

As we walk in these five aspects of courage, we will be

able to Man UP and take the steps we need to take. We can go through the fires of life and not get burned. We will come out and not even smell like smoke. We need to meditate on these five principles of courage until they become an essential part of our being!

The sin, singular sin, that so easily ensnares us is **discouragement**. When we get discouraged, it's because we have lost our focus on the fact that God is with us, and we forgot to Man UP and use our faith. We cannot run the race if we do not Man UP. We will not be able to do anything positive at all. Discouragement is not just a bad feeling; it violates the Man UP mandate to be strong and courageous!

A Great Reward

Do not, therefore, fling away your fearless confidence, for it carries a great and glorious compensation of reward (Hebrews 10:35 AMP).

There's those words again: **great reward**! What is our reward? Anything the covenant offers! Whatever it is we are fighting for—our homes, our families, our health, our jobs—whatever we need is our great reward because we Man UP and know that God is with us. We know this because of our relationship with Jesus Christ, our Savior!

The Man UP mandate calls us to take courage and accomplish supernatural results. We can tap into all the power of our manhood and arise to greatness.

I can sense your excitement over the truth that you are called to greatness. Man UP and take courage and read further. You are embarking on a journey of courageous living and will receive its great rewards!

Chapter 3

The Leading Man

The director grabbed the megaphone and shouted "Lights, Camera, Action!" The actors took their positions and began performing their roles according to the script. Under the director's instructions, the bestselling book, *Man UP: The Power To Release the Champion in You*, was being made into a blockbuster movie.

Did you know that you are playing the leading man in this blockbuster hit? This is real life, not a fairy tale. This is really happening. You are the leading man in the movie, *Man UP*. This is your life with all the drama, action, and comedy to make it a success. In this blockbuster, you will be directed to have courage. Some of the scenes will demand compassion, while others will demand wisdom and strength. In the different scenes of this blockbuster, you will be called upon to perform as a fireman, rain man, repairman, a military man, a political man, and even Superman. We'll discuss each one of these in greater detail. Let's start with the leading man role first.

Leading Man Backdrop

Let's look at the backdrop for your role as leading man as we get the action started. We find the backdrop in Psalm 139:1, 4, 14-16.

*Lord, you have examined my heart and know everything about me. You know what I am going to say even before I say it, Thank you for making me so wonderfully complex! Your workmanship is marvelous—and how well I know it. You watched me as I was being formed in utter seclusion, as I was woven together in the dark of the womb. You saw me before I was born. **Every day of my life was recorded in your book. Every moment was laid out before a single day had passed*** (emphasis added).

Backdrop Scriptures reveal important truths God wants you to understand about His script for you as leading man. The Bible says that God knows the plans He has for your future, and they are full of hope and goodness (Jeremiah 29:11). What God has planned for you is beyond what you could ask or think (Ephesians 3:20). These Scriptures tell us that the book of your life was already written by God before you were even on your parents' minds.

You are important because God knows you! God knows each of us! He planned our arrival on earth, and every day of our life is scripted by Him. Even if your arrival was less than into perfect circumstances (remember He was born in a stable), God has written a bestseller of your life story. You have the opportunity to either discover it and follow the script or ignore it altogether.

One man was conceived during the rape of his mother.

She abandoned him as a baby, and he was an orphan. But this man, James Robison, discovered that God knows him and has a bestselling script written for every day of his life.

We all want to know ourselves, and we want others to know us. But God says He really knows us! He knows everything, and He has so many thoughts about us that we can't even count them. He knows our strengths and our weaknesses, and He has written this whole story based on them to build some tension into the plot of the book of our lives and cause us to become more than we were before. Review the backdrop scenario in Psalm 139:1-18 to see some great truths about your role in the bestseller movie, *Man UP*.

Embrace the Drama

God has written drama and comedy into our life stories, and we need to embrace them rather than worry about them. A good screenwriter looks for an excellent book that he already knows is successful in order to make a good movie. The director and/or the screenwriter then will insert some twists in the plot and some surprises along with some tense moments. The goal is to get viewers to become involved and to say, "What's going to happen next?" When it comes to our life stories, we need to remind ourselves this is just a movie of the book God has already written for our lives. We can check the script and enjoy the process.

The Script

Moses understood that the book had already been written and that he was just acting out the role of leading man. Hear what Moses said about the script: *"But now, please forgive their sin—and if not, then blot me out of your book you have written"* (Exodus 32:32 NIV). Moses understood that God is not writing the book as He goes along or as our life develops. God has written this book before we were ever conceived. What happens is that God has to blot out from our lives (our role as leading men) the parts of the script to which we will not submit.

When we become born again, God does not write our names into the Lamb's Book of Life. Our names were already written down in the Lamb's Book of Life when Jesus died and rose from the dead. (See Philippians 4:3, Revelation 17:8; 22:19.) *"For God so loved the world, that he gave his only begotten Son, that whosoever believeth in Him should not perish, but have everlasting life"* (John 3:16 KJV). However, if we do not accept what has already been written, then God must blot our names out of the Book. Let me explain further about our role.

Accepting Your Role

Your name is written in the Book of Life, but will you accept it? If you die without accepting Jesus as your personal Savior, then God must blot your name out of the Book of Life. *"All who are victorious will be clothed in white. I will never erase their names from the Book of Life, but I will announce before my Father and his angels that they are mine"* (Revelation 3:5 NLT).

On judgment day the book of our lives (one of the books John saw in Revelation 20) will be opened, and we will be judged on how we accomplished the script God has written for our lives. *"I saw the dead, both great and small, standing before God's throne. And the books were opened, including the Book of Life. And the dead were judged according to the things written in the books, according to what they had done"* (Revelation 20:12 NLT).

We can rejoice if we have accepted the salvation Jesus purchased for us. We will shout about what we overcame as we are rewarded. We will rejoice over the dreams that were accomplished and birthed through adversity. Even Jesus learned obedience by the things He suffered that were scripted for Him. He embraced the drama of His life. We can Man UP and deal with the drama and comedy of our lives. We do not have to numb ourselves to the pain in life. We can embrace it because God has written the book, and we are acting it out in the movie.

A Blockbuster Movie

My Hollywood friends tell me that to have a good movie you must have a good writer, a good director, and a good editor. If you have a good script and director, you can use mediocre actors and still have a great movie if you also have a good editor.

The Holy Spirit is the director of our role as leading man, giving us instruction and guidance. If we will listen to our director, He will tell us what the scene of the day involves. He may say, "You will need to swing on a rope over a lion's den and then run through a fire and so forth," and then ask, "Do you want the thrill of this, or do you want a stunt double?" Greater rewards are available for those who perform their own stunts. Generations will talk about them forever.

People still talk about Daniel and the lion's den today because he embraced the thrill of his role as leading man and performed his own stunts. The Holy Spirit, our director, will tell us if we are doing a good job or if we need to do a retake of the scene until we get the cut that He wants for the movie.

Jesus is the editor of the movie (our lives), and He has full authority to rewrite any scene. An example of divine editing is recorded in Romans 4:20 where it says that Abraham was a man who never wavered in the faith. However, if we go back and read the story of Abraham, it appears he did waver. When the king wanted to sleep with his wife, Abraham panicked; he said that she was his sister and to go ahead (Genesis 12). What kind of unwavering faith is that? However, Jesus, our editor, fixes the final version of the movie and says, "Abraham never wavered!"

When we stand before God and He says, "Well done," it won't be because we were wonderful and perfect all the time. It will be because the editor has done some work on us! Our life's story has been written by God. We are just acting out the role as leading man. The Holy Spirit is directing the movie, and Jesus will do the final editing. Praise the Lord!

If you are having a rotten time, maybe you have picked up the wrong script. Check out the Book that God has written. It is an exciting story, and you will want to enjoy the thrill of it as the Holy Spirit directs you. Let me explain how this works.

From Bestseller to Blockbuster

Here is how the making of the movie of your life works. Romans 10:17 (NKJV) says, *"Faith comes by hearing, and hearing by the Word of God."* When I have studied the written Word of God (the script) and hidden His Word in my heart, then I am ready to hear the Holy Spirit speak to me and live by faith in His directions. Faith comes because I have the Word of God hidden in my heart. That gives me the confidence to hear the Holy Spirit's directions and by faith to obey them. The result is that the daily chapter of the book that God has written about my life will be lived out by me each day. I will be acting out the movie version of the bestseller, *Man UP: The Power To Release the Champion in You!*

Jesus gave us a scene of how this happens in the gospel of Luke. The book containing the messages of Isaiah the prophet was handed to Jesus, and He opened it to the place where it says:

> *The Spirit of the Lord is upon me, for he has appointed me to preach Good News to the poor. He has sent me to proclaim that captives will be released, that the blind will see, that the downtrodden will be freed from their oppressors, and that the time of the Lord's favor has come."* He *closed the book, handed it back to the attendant, and sat down . . . Then Jesus said, "This scripture has come true today before your very eyes!"* (Luke 4:17-21 TLB).

Jesus acted out the scene that was written. It was fulfilled that very day.

In our lives, we receive God's direction in our hearts. We hear the Holy Spirit speak when we have God's Word hidden there. We have confidence that we have heard from the Holy Spirit because our hearts do not condemn us. Therefore, we act out the directions of the Holy Spirit.

If we do not follow the director's instructions, however,

then God, the writer of the script, goes to the editor, and our editor fixes the scene. *The Lord will work out His plans for my life* (Psalm 138:8 NLT).

Lights, Camera, Action!

When we are acting out our role as leading man, first the director calls for *lights*. This is when we receive the revelation of instructions from the Holy Spirit, our director. Next, there is the call for *camera*. This is for us to get our focus in perspective. We focus on the truth that God has written the script, and we are just acting out the movie. We focus on what the scene of the day calls for. Then the final call is *action*. We act out our part in the movie. The result is a blockbuster hit. You may not receive an Academy Award, but you will receive a heavenly reward!

Enjoy the thrill of being the leading man in the script God has written of your life. Become best friends with your director, the Holy Spirit. He will lead you into great and mighty things of which you know not! Don't panic over dumb mistakes. Maintain fellowship with your director, and He will have the editor fix the final cut!

Many men who have excelled in their roles as leading men have had stars with their names on it placed in Hollywood's famous walk of fame. But we have an opportunity to be listed in God's walk of fame. How well we reflect Jesus Christ in the drama or comedy of life can cause others to remember us (see Hebrews 11:30-40) or forget us.

Every blockbuster has a plot. If the movie is going to be any good, it must contain scenes of adversity as well as scenes of success for the leading character. The story of our lives, written in advance by God, contains adversity and prosperity. We must understand the role of both for our walk of fame through life.

Any problems we experience contain a gold mine of wisdom, opportunity, and potential promotion. It is up to us to discern the hidden value of the problems. Ecclesiastes 7:10-14 says,

> *Don't long for "the good old days," for you don't know whether they were any better than today. Being wise is as good as being rich; in fact, it is better. Wisdom or money can get you almost anything, but it's important to know that only wisdom can save your life. Notice the way God does things; then fall into line. Don't fight the ways of God, for who can straighten out what he has made crooked? Enjoy prosperity while you can. But when hard times strike, realize that both come from God. That way you will realize that nothing is certain in this life* (NLT).

In the above Scriptures, Solomon instructs us to remember that God uses adversity and promotion to teach us to lean entirely on Him. We often run from affliction and view it as a lack of faith. We must remember that God uses hardship in our lives. Any problem we face could be a godsend of opportunity. When Pharaoh faced depression, Joseph entered the scene. When King Saul was tormented by evil spirits, David entered. When his countrymen faced annihilation, Jepthah re-entered. Problems are keys to change and potential promotion.

Solving problems can create new relationships. David married the daughter of the king by solving the problem of Goliath. Abraham's servant needed water for his camels; this problem led to his meeting with Rachel, who would become Isaac's wife. The famine activated Naomi's move to Bethlehem. There, Ruth met Boaz from whose lineage would come Jesus. Problems can bring changes to your life. Pharaoh gave the position of prime minister to Joseph after he solved the unexplained dream. Problems can be the key to recognition and promotion. When the king experienced great anger and depression over a forgotten dream, it proved to be Daniel's opportunity for promotion.

We must always look at a problem as an opening to rise to significance as a leading man. Setbacks are seeds that grow into great harvests. We should not run from a problem. We should embrace the drama and increase in greatness (Matthew 11:11). Solomon understood trials. He instructed us to notice the way God works. He wanted us to understand that adversity and prosperity are both ways God uses to teach us to lean entirely on Him. Whatever the scene of the day calls for, you can Man UP and enjoy the process.

Remembered by Your Role

Many of us remember the infamous names of Adolph Hitler, Stalin, and Mussolini. They are remembered by millions because of the devastating problems they created in the world. We may be remembered as a problem, or we may be remembered as a solution. Goliath is thought of as the problem; David is recognized as the solution. When the plot of our life's story includes hardship, don't forget that this is a chance to reveal our distinction from others. Joseph is remembered because he solved the problem of provision during famine. We will be remembered either for the problems we solve or the ones we create.

Our lives are a movie for all to remember. How we respond to times of adversity or prosperity positions us for greatness or mediocrity in life. God has already written our life stories, and we can rise to greatness (see Matthew 11:11; 5:19). How we handle good times and bad will be remembered. How you respond to life will become the movie version of the book God has written of your life.

Corrections From the Director

Correction was a major part of the ministry of Jesus. In the following passage, Jesus corrected Peter:

> *But He turned, and said unto Peter, Get thee behind Me, Satan: thou art an offence unto me: for thou savourest not the things that be of God, but those that be of men* (Matthew 16:23 KJV).

Jesus corrected the disciples as well.

> *Later He appeared to the eleven as they sat at the table; and He rebuked their unbelief and hardness of heart, because they did not believe those who had seen Him after He had risen* (Mark 16:14).

Correction is also a major part of the ministry of our director, the Holy Spirit. Jesus does not say that the Holy Spirit will *control* us, and He does not say that the Holy Spirit will *force* us to do anything. He does say that the Holy Spirit will *direct* us.

> *But when He, the Spirit of truth, comes, He will direct you into all truth; for He will not speak on His own*

initiative, but whatever He hears, He will speak; and He will disclose to you what is to come (John 16:13).

A good book or movie involves many scene changes. We are instructed to embrace each new scene with courage by forgetting yesterday and courageously pressing on while trusting our director's instructions. Philippians 3:12 (TLB) says,

I don't mean to say that I have already achieved these things or that I have already reached perfection! But I keep working toward the day when I will finally be all that Christ Jesus saves me for.

To have a blockbuster movie of our starring roles as leading men, we must follow the director's instructions and corrections. This will bring great value to the many people who will be not only entertained, but also enlightened and encouraged by the drama of our lives. How well we follow the director determines our chance for promotion in life. Accepting direction is the difference between maturity and immaturity. It can mean the difference between producing a flop and a blockbuster hit.

And the Winner Is . . .

I have great news: you have been nominated for an award far greater than any Oscar or Emmy. Even better, your peers and movie watchers do not have a vote that they can use against you, nor can they rate your performance. You have been nominated for a heavenly award as the Leading Man in the Best Picture, *Man UP.*

Have you ever watched the Academy Awards? Do you remember waiting with anticipation for the presenters to announce the best leading man or the picture of the year? I remember waiting with baited breath to hear the presenter open the envelope while saying, "And the winner is . . ."

Your nomination for Best Leading Man has been announced (Matthew 6:6; 1 Corinthians 3:14; Revelation 22:12). You are starring in a blockbuster. By following the directions of the Holy Spirit, you can embrace every scene with confidence. You can enjoy the comedy and the drama of life with peace through intimacy with the Holy Spirit. Enjoy your role. You are becoming a winner. I can hear the heavenly announcer say, "And the winner is . . . you!"

Award winning actors always research the roles they are about to play. The following chapters will give you valuable insight into the roles you will be playing as the leading man in the blockbuster movie of your life, *Man UP.*

Chapter 4

The Sexual Man

Would you tell your wife if you were ever approached by a hooker? I recall an incident that happened when I was traveling with Dr. Ed Cole for one of his men's ministry events. While in the elevator going to the conference room, two beautiful women entered and stood on each side of Dr. Cole. One of the lovely ladies began to rub his head and said, "I love bald men. They are so sexy!"

On another occasion, I was with my wife waiting to get on the elevator at our hotel when we were approached by a gorgeous young lady. She made us a bold offer for the evening, and we instantly realized that she was a hooker.

Some men may fantasize about situations like those just described, but they are deadly traps. In case you are wondering what happened in the two situations above, Dr. Cole thanked the ladies for their compliment, told them that Jesus loved them, and stepped out of the elevator. I didn't have time to think about telling the young lady about Jesus because my wife had an instant message for her and for me!

Manhood has many demands placed on it throughout our

lifetime. While performing as leading men in the movies of our lives, our sexuality will always be on display. True manhood cries out for genuine intimacy. Our souls long for a vital connection to a mate, and many men go through multiple marriages trying to find it. I have journeyed from the inability to be intimate to a place of deep intimacy and great fulfillment with my wife, Darlene.

What surprised me the most was that understanding all the "sexual secrets" is not the secret to true intimacy and fulfillment. As I understood the meaning of covenant and who the Holy Spirit really is, my entire life was changed and my ability for intimacy greatly enhanced.

In this chapter on the sexual man, I want to share the discoveries I made on this journey of sexuality and fulfillment. It began when I discovered that God loves me and is for me, not against me. Let me take you on a quick trip down this road of discovery to truly fulfilled manhood and the ability to experience true intimacy.

God's Covenant

God is a God of covenant. While it is not my purpose to explain covenant, a thorough understanding of the conditions of a blood covenant will greatly assist us in our sexual discoveries. Covenant is based on strengths and weaknesses. I share your strengths and your weaknesses, and you share mine.

When God made a covenant with Abraham, the father of our faith, the sign of this covenant was circumcision. Circumcision was the seal of the primary agreement between Israel and God Himself. Circumcision is not natural to man. Man is naturally born uncircumcised. Circumcision as the sign of the covenant required by God, by its very nature, points to the unnaturalness of God's standard for man. What God requires of man is not natural to man. Men had to decide to go against nature and become circumcised. This illustrates that for man to have covenant with God is contrary to nature. Genesis 17:11 says, *"And you shall be circumcised in the flesh of your foreskins, and it shall be a sign of the covenant between me and you."* With the establishment of this covenant, a covenant that is contrary to nature, humanity is put on notice of just what God's standards are.

What is natural to me as a man, in regards to my sexual journey through life, may not be what God desires or requires. God's design for my sexuality will bring true fulfillment because God is love. God is for me; He is not against me. Let's talk about the sexual desires that are natural for us as men but may be traps to deny us the ability to Man UP.

Samson, the world's strongest man, had a natural sexual desire that became a weakness to his manhood and cost him everything (Judges 15:14-15; 16:20). Samson's power was the anointing of the Holy Spirit. This anointing manifested itself in unusual physical strength. Samson fell in lust with Delilah. I use the word *lust* and not *love* because love gives and lust gets. Love satisfies you at my expense, and lust satisfies me at your expense. Delilah was a trap to discover the secret to Samson's strength. Samson gave away his secret of the anointing and with it his great physical strength. Judges 16:20 tells us that Samson felt nothing different at that time and did not know that his strength had left him until it was too late.

For all we know, this loss of anointing and physical strength may have been an unconscious diminishing during the time he foolishly acted out his natural desires for sex with Delilah. What we do know is that when his head was shaved, his strength utterly left him. He lost the anointing and didn't know it until it was too late. This is an example of what the Bible calls grieving the Holy Spirit (Ephesians 4:30 NIV). When the Holy Spirit is grieved and departs like this, it doesn't mean we have lost our salvation. We have been sealed for the day of redemption. Paul said in Ephesians 4:30, *"And do not grieve the Holy Spirit of God, with whom you were sealed for the day of redemption."* At the end of his life, Samson received his anointing back and accomplished more *"when he died than while he lived"* (Judges 16:30). I want to help men maintain the Man UP anointing throughout *all* of their lives. In this chapter, I want to share how this may be accomplished.

I had a supernatural experience that revolutionized my idea of intimacy. Before I share this experience with you, I think it will be beneficial if we understand the process in which I was involved. I was searching for victory over the flesh and power that seemed to be missing in my manhood. I heard a lot about sin and how rotten we are as men, but I didn't hear much about how to have victory or a pure sexuality as a man. Praise the Lord, I discovered six steps to intimacy with the Holy Spirit. My understanding of sin and my sexuality finally made sense. It is through this intimacy with the Holy Spirit that I discovered how to Man UP and release the power for manhood.

The Man UP Trap

Before we take a specific look at the six steps of intimacy, let's get a clear understanding of sin because sin is the Man

UP trap. Scripture teaches that all men are born sinners and must be born again to enter the kingdom of God. This is the very first step to being able to Man UP. Sin is natural to man. When the Bible refers to the flesh, it is usually talking about that which is natural to man. Sin may be described as that which falls short of or misses the mark of God's standard for man. Sin is what makes it impossible to Man UP. Romans 3:23 says, *"For all have sinned and come short of the glory of God."* Mankind has proven helpless to Man UP and change his sinful nature that is natural to him. Jeremiah 13:23 says, *"Can the Ethiopian change his skin or the leopard its spots? Neither can you do good who are accustomed to doing evil."*

Sin is often referred to in the Bible as a snare. It may be natural to man, but it is a snare. Many passages in both the Old and New Testaments illustrate how sin is self-reinforcing, leading to an ever deeper entanglement. Scripture indicates that the snare of sin is that it begins as appearing harmless because it is natural for man to behave in a way that is contrary to God's standard. Then this behavior eventually reveals its power over the will. Man denies the potential for entrapment, inadvertently ensuring that he will not have the ability to Man UP because, like Samson, he is trapped. Proverbs 5:22-23 says,

> *His own iniquities entrap the wicked man, and he is caught in the cords of his sin. He shall die for lack of instruction, and in the greatness of his folly he shall go astray.*

Second Peter 2:19 tells us,

> *While they promise them liberty, they themselves are*

slaves of corruption; for by whom a person is overcome, by him also he is brought into bondage."

Modern psychology of compulsive behavior has learned that when a man is mastered by his desires, denial takes over as a specific mechanism; this subverts any lingering suspicion that escape is even desirable. What is actually a frightening vice is disguised as a virtue. The prophet describes this state of blindness in Jeremiah 17:9, *"The heart is deceitful above all things, and desperately wicked; who can know it?"*

According to the American Psychiatric Association if we repeat a behavior enough times that behavior actually gets burned into our psyche through the synaptic connections of our brain (*American Journal of Public Health, Neurocomputing: Foundations of Research*, Dr. Jeffrey Satinover, American Psychiatric Association). The behavior then becomes our master (like Samson's addiction to Delilah) and without supernatural assistance is not likely to be overcome.

When a man realizes the truth of his soul's condition as compared to God's standard for him, he feels helpless and doomed to his learned behavior. But there is an answer. We can discover how to Man UP and overcome what is natural but deadly to man. The Apostle Paul describes this helpless doomed condition of the natural man.

> *For what I am doing, I do not understand. For what I will to do, that I do not practice; but what I hate, that I do . . . But now, it is no longer I who do it, but sin that dwells in me. For I know that in me (that is, in my flesh) nothing good dwells; for to will is present with me, but how to perform what is good I do not find . . . For I delight in the law of God according to the inward man.*

But I see another law in my members, warring against the law of my mind, and bringing me into captivity to the law of sin which is in my members. O wretched man that I am! Who will deliver me from this body of death? (Romans 7:15-24).

This is the heart cry of man: "How can I Man UP? Who will help me to Man UP? I want to Man UP, but I can't!"

Israel's history following the establishment of covenant with God is one of continual failure to meet God's requirements. Like the Apostle Paul, they needed a Savior to rescue them. Today is no different. It is not natural for man to meet God's requirements and Man UP. We make the same statement and ask the same question, "What a wretched person I am. Who will rescue me from this body of death?" Divine intervention is needed!

David understood this same condition of an inability to Man UP. David said that sin is defined by God, not by nature or what is natural to man. Sin is not against nature; sin is against God. David said in Psalm 51:4 *"Against You, You only, have I sinned, and done this evil in your sight—that you may be found just when you speak, and blameless when you judge."*

So natural is sin, and so unnatural are God's requirements, that much of the Bible tells the story of man's inability to obey these requirements through his own natural effort. The Bible shows the desperate human need for supernatural assistance in living any kind of a godly lifestyle. Ecclesiastes 7:20 says, *"For there is not a just man on earth who does good, and does not sin."*

Because God knows how unnatural it is for us not to sin, He refrains from swift, harsh judgment and tempers His response with patience and mercy. David explains this in Psalm 103:10-14.

> *He has not dealt with us according to our sins, nor punished us according to our iniquities. For as the heavens are high above the earth, So great is His mercy toward those who fear Him; as far as the east is from the west, So far has He removed our transgressions from us, as a father pities his children, So the LORD pities those who fear Him. For He knows our frame; He remembers that we are dust.*

Without an understanding of and dependence on God's Word, we cannot address right and wrong. Science alone cannot determine what is right and what is wrong. If we view only what is natural as right, we will end up in destruction. We resist the sin that is natural to us only with the greatest effort. Our efforts to Man UP require the guidance of God's Word **and a Savior who empowers us with His Holy Spirit** to achieve any success! This is what David discovered after his adulterous affair that ended in murder. He writes in Psalm 119:11-17,

> *Your word I have hidden in my heart, that I might not sin against you. Blessed are You, O LORD! Teach me your statutes. With my lips I have declared all the judgments of your mouth. I have rejoiced in the way of your testimonies, as much as in all riches. I will meditate on your precepts, and contemplate your ways. I will delight myself in your statutes; I will not forget your word. Deal bountifully with your servant, that I may live and keep your word.*

The Power To Man UP

The power to overcome the natural desires of the flesh, whatever they may be, does not come from nature, nor from men themselves as a matter of simple choice, but rather from the Holy Spirit. (We will discuss this power in the Superman chapter.)

To live as a free man, who is empowered in all the dimensions of life, we need the gift our Savior gave to us, namely the Holy Spirit in us and upon us. It is what goes into something that determines what comes out of that something. We should not try to get the bad out of us; we need to get the good into us. Scripture says we are destroyed for lack of knowledge (Hosea 4:6). We need to get God's wisdom into us. Scripture says that we cleanse our ways by getting the Word of God into us. It is only through the Holy Spirit in us and upon us that He empowers us with what we need and removes what needs to be removed (Psalm 119:9-12; 103:8-12).

Scripture says we are God's workmanship. We are a work of God in process. When we recognize and admit our inadequacy to be able to Man UP in our own power, we can turn from prideful dependence on ourselves to voluntary dependence on God. We learn to receive the Holy Spirit in us and upon us, and turn our focus on Him.

Man's original sin was and is that our pride wants to decide for ourselves what is good and what is evil. We want independence from God. Sadly, independence from God means dependence upon our natural desires, and the result of this is destruction. Only God through His Holy Spirit can bring us to a conviction of the sin of our natural desires. Then we need to depend on God supernaturally to give us a new nature with new desires and the ability to Man UP. We must grow in strength, discipline, and intimacy as we practice these new desires. All of this is a process. We are His workmanship. We are men being worked on by God.

If we cry out to God for His salvation, then what we become is the result of His workmanship. I can trust Him to complete the work He has started in you and in me. **I need to accept you, and I need you to accept me** for where we are in this process of His workmanship. *"For we are his workmanship, created in Christ Jesus unto good works, which God hath before ordained that we should walk in them"* (Ephesians 2:10).

Like the apostle Paul, I have become convinced. *"For I am persuaded that neither death nor life, nor angels nor principalities nor powers, nor things present nor things to come, nor height nor depth, nor any other created thing, shall be able to separate us from the love of God which is in Christ Jesus our Lord"* (Romans 8:38-39). Therefore, I trust the Lord to complete His workmanship in me, and I've learned to enjoy this journey of intimacy and empowering.

Victory over our fleshly desires must begin with a desire in our hearts to want to please our Lord and Savior, Jesus Christ. If it is our heart's desire to walk worthy of the high calling of Jesus Christ and learn the ability to Man UP, we will want to maintain intimacy with the Holy Spirit every day. **It is only through daily intimacy with the Holy Spirit that any inner improvement takes place in man.** I have discovered that the Holy Spirit is a real person, not just a presence. The Holy Spirit is the secret to discovering intimacy, purpose, and fulfillment in life, and the only real power to change anything. Every person is in a different place in his or her sexuality and relationship with the Holy Spirit. Love will simply encourage us to cultivate intimacy with the Holy Spirit and pray for one another.

It is the Holy Spirit who conforms us to the image of Jesus Christ. Therefore, I want to offer steps of intimacy that have helped me cultivate my relationship with the Holy Spirit. This is not to say I have arrived, but to offer tools for your consideration as you desire greater intimacy with the Holy Spirit and empowerment to understand your sexuality, relieve suffering and emptiness, and increase joy in yourself and others.

Many who have adapted these steps and allowed God to work through them have been surprised by the noticeable improvements. They have reported progress in their awareness, their sensitivity, and their ability to love and to be free. I pray that God will grant you the courage to work and cultivate intimacy with the Holy Spirit.

Six Steps of Intimacy

1. The first step to intimacy is to **admit that I am powerless apart from God**, and parts of my life want to be unmanageable. Read Romans 7:18,

I know nothing good lives in me, that is, in my sinful nature. For I have the desire to do what is good, but I cannot carry it out.

The idea that there are areas of our lives over which we are powerless may be a new concept for us. This does not lessen the impact of our salvation. The Bible is full of accounts of people who struggled continually to overcome past mistakes, the weaknesses of their human nature, and life's many temptations.

The great Apostle Paul describes his desperate powerlessness and unmanageability of his life in the verse we just read from Romans. His acknowledgment of this powerlessness does not interfere with his commitment to do God's will. When we stop finding excuses for our behavior, we have taken the first step toward achieving intimacy and humility to accept spiritual help from the Holy Spirit.

2. The second step is **coming to the place where I believe the Holy Spirit has the power to restore me to wholeness and conform me to the image of Jesus Christ.** Believing in God does not always mean that we accept His power. *"For it's God who works in you to will and to act according to his good purpose"* (Philippians 2:13). As we become more dependent on the Holy Spirit, the quality of our lives will improve. *"Not that we are competent to claim anything for ourselves, but our competence comes from God"* (2 Corinthians 3:5).

> *So do not fear for I am with you; do not be dismayed, for I am your God. I will strengthen and help you; I will uphold you with my righteous right hand* (Isaiah 41:10).

3. The third step is to **stir up my courage and honestly confess my fears and inadequacies.** When cleaning my bedroom closet at home, I take a personal inventory of what I have in order to know what needs to be kept and what needs to be discarded. Clothes can trigger memories of the past, so my inventory may bring up both good and bad memories. To effectively deal with the closet, though, I cannot let these memories determine what I do with the clothes.

In the same way in my life, the past is not to be dwelled

on; it simply serves as a tool to help me understand my current condition. As I look honestly at myself, I become aware of areas that need to be strengthened or changed. I confess to the Holy Spirit exactly how I feel about trusting Him. I ask Him to search me and reveal to me anything that is offensive to Him.

> *Search me, O God, and know my heart; test me and know my anxious thoughts. See if there is any offensive way in me, and lead me in the way everlasting"* (Psalm 139:23-24).

When I realize that God already knows all my faults, then I must face the fear that this evokes. *"There is no fear in love. But perfect love drives out fear, because fear has to do with punishment. The man who fears is not made perfect in love"* (1 John 4:18). My emotions may try to run away as I get honest about my life. I must remember God's promise in Lamentations 3:19-22,

> *I remember my affliction and my wandering, the bitterness and the gall. I well remember them, and my soul is downcast within me. Yet this I call to mind and therefore I have hope: because of the Lord's great love we are not consumed, for His compassions never fail.*

This process of my relationship with the Holy Spirit enables me to accept myself where I am and trust the Holy Spirit to work in me to accomplish His pleasure. I understand that this is not a quick fix but a process. I choose to submit to the Holy Spirit working in me, knowing that He has only good plans for my future (see Jeremiah 29:11).

I should not blame God or others for what has happened

to me, but I need to accept my history for what it is. This increases my intimacy with the Holy Spirit, and I begin to trust Him and accept His love unconditionally. I have humbled myself before the Lord, and now He will lift me up (see James 4:10). If I am willing to let the Holy Spirit work in my life to conform me to the image of Jesus Christ, He will never leave me nor forsake me. I am not expected to remove any character defects alone; I am only expected to let go and let God do it. Through this willingness to let God be in control, I learn to trust Him more completely.

4. The fourth step is **remaining open to whatever instrument the Holy Spirit may want to use to minister to me.** I have learned that God will never remove anything I need. In fact, He adds to my life. God gives grace to the humble, but He resists the proud. God gives grace through other people as well as directly to me through prayer and meditation. God often uses outside forces as He conforms me to the image of Jesus Christ. Ministers, teachers, doctors, and others can all be instruments of God's grace.

As I cultivate intimacy with the Holy Spirit, I must remain open to whatever avenue He chooses to minister His grace to me. As I maintain this humble dependence on the Holy Spirit, I have found that I gain more power to overcome all sin and iniquity.

> *Good and upright is the Lord; therefore he instructs sinners in his ways. He guides the humble in what is right and teaches them his way. All the ways of the Lord are loving and faithful for those who keep the demands of his covenant. For the sake of your name, O Lord, forgive my iniquity, though it be great* (Psalm 25:8-11).

But he gives us more grace. That is why Scripture says: "God opposes the proud but gives grace to the humble." Submit yourselves, then, to God. Resist the devil and he will flee from you. Come near to God and he will come near to you (James 4:6-7 NIV).

5. The fifth step I have learned is that **a daily regimen of prayer and Bible reading is crucial to experiencing intimacy with the Holy Spirit.** *"Let the word of Christ dwell in you richly"* (Colossians 3:16). Each day I ask God for direction in my thoughts and actions. I ask Him to keep me free from self-pity, dishonesty, and selfishness. I ask for His wisdom and guidance to take care of any problems. I surround myself as much as possible with praise and worship music. There is a power released through praise and worship and purification as I thank God for His love and guidance in my life. I need this power and purification daily, and I do not hesitate to ask for it.

I strongly encourage you to be conscious of what you are seeing and hearing daily. It makes a difference in the quality of life you will enjoy. Sing to yourself. Make a new song about what you are learning from reading the Bible and sing it to yourself. As you surround yourself with praise and worship, you will experience a release of power to Man UP and overcome.

6. The sixth step is to remind myself that **everything in the kingdom of God operates on the seed principle.** That means everything happens in stages and not all at once. Miracles do happen, but the norm of life happens in due process. Don't get impatient. Thank God daily for even the little successes you experience. You are His workmanship, and

He will finish the work you have allowed Him to begin in your life.

As you experience growing in intimacy with the Holy Spirit, remember we are all in the transformation process.

At one time we too were foolish, disobedient, deceived and enslaved by all kinds of passions and pleasures. We lived in malice and envy, being hated and hating one another. But when the kindness and love of God our Savior appeared, he saved us, not because of righteous things we had done, but because of his mercy. He saved us through the washing of rebirth and renewal by the Holy Spirit, whom he poured out on us generously through Jesus Christ our Savior, so that, having been justified by his grace, we might become heirs having the hope of eternal life (Titus 3:3-7 NIV).

My Unforgettable Encounter

While practicing these steps at the peak of my pastoral career, I had a unique supernatural experience. My life was dramatically changed in August 1986. While I was in bed in the early morning hours, I had a supernatural visitation. Jesus appeared to me and stood me to my feet. He placed my hands against His hands, and we stood nose to nose. Without speaking a word, the Spirit of the Lord passed completely through me.

As I sought to understand this dramatic experience, I spoke with Dr. Oral Roberts, Dr. Lester Sumrall, and others who are spiritual leaders in my life. Their counsel was of great help. I think what I experienced could best be described as a vision. I am not comfortable sharing much detail about this experience except that when I say Jesus appeared to me, I knew it was Him. He did not introduce Himself as such, but I just had a knowing. What was unusual for me was that He had no facial features. All I saw was pure light when I looked into His face. Those I spoke to for counsel and many others since have told me that this is not uncommon. The Holy Spirit often reveals Himself, and because we have never seen a spirit, we think it is Jesus Christ (who had a flesh body); but that is why there were no facial features.

Before you think I am over the deep end, let me assure you that this was my burning bush experience, and I am not trying to build any doctrine on it. God did do this type of thing throughout the Bible. God did this for Paul when his name was Saul on the road to Damascus. He did it for Peter when He sent an angel to the prison while the church prayed for him. Jacob had an uncommon experience at Bethel where he wrestled with an angel of the Lord. We will discuss other life-changing Holy Spirit experiences in later chapters.

God creates unforgettable encounters. The purpose of an encounter is not just for an experience. It should bring you to the person of the Holy Spirit. It should cause you to fall in love with the Holy Spirit as a person and not an experience. If it doesn't bond you with the Holy Spirit, it was just an experience. Your life should change from this encounter, and a journey of intimacy with the Holy Spirit will begin.

The Holy Spirit does not want His gifts and manifestations to mesmerize us or become our focus. The Holy Spirit wants us to listen to Him continuously to communicate and focus on His presence with us. Whatever stresses we have in life, whether we think we need more money, a new relationship, or a new house, etc., it is the Holy Spirit that we are searching for and need. The Holy Spirit is called the "Spirit of Wisdom" (Isaiah 11:2). What we need is His wisdom to get us to where we need to be.

The Holy Spirit created us. He formed us. He skillfully sculptured our life. We are empty unless He enters our lives. We are blind unless He opens our eyes. We are deaf to the incredible sounds on earth unless He unlocks our ears. He is whom we seek. He is a gift from Jesus Christ who told us that the Holy Spirit would continue His ministry on earth while He reigned in heaven. He will satisfy us beyond our imagination! To Man UP necessitates that we cultivate an intimate relationship with the Holy Spirit.

The Man UP Mentor

Jesus taught, *"And I will pray the father, and He shall give you another Helper, that He may abide with you forever"* (John 14:16). The Holy Spirit is not an it; He is a person, not merely a presence. He is a person who talks, thinks, plans, and is incredibly brilliant and articulate. Jesus taught that the Holy Spirit is much more than a presence. The aroma is not really the food. The stink is not the skunk! The quack is not the duck. The Holy Spirit's presence is proof of His person-hood (John 16:13).

Jesus recognized the Holy Spirit as a mentor. *"He shall teach you all things"* (John 14:26). The Holy Spirit uses various pictures of Himself to reveal His workings, His nature, and various qualities about Him. In order to Man UP, we need to be mentored by the Holy Spirit.

The Holy Spirit can enter our lives like water, refreshing

us. The Holy Spirit can enter our lives like fire, purifying us. The Holy Spirit can move suddenly and quickly in our lives, like wind (Isaiah 44:3-4, Acts 2:2-4). The Holy Spirit will come to us the way we need Him the most. He can come as a gentle nurturer, like a mother caring for her dependent child. He can come as a brilliant and articulate advisor when we are facing a difficult decision. He can come as a comforting healer when we have been scarred and tormented from a battle.

The Holy Spirit is a person. We should not attempt to Man UP without an intimate relationship with the Holy Spirit. We cannot truly know love without Him. He is the one who sheds the love of God abroad in our hearts (Romans 5:5). The Holy Spirit desires to be our mentor and empower us to discover purpose and fulfillment in life.

The Champion Connection

Man is the Holy Spirit's greatest product (Job 33:4). Our personality, body, and everything about us is the design of the Holy Spirit (Psalm 139:14). Our body is the temple of the Holy Spirit (1 Corinthians 6:19). The Holy Spirit is the Spirit of life within us that keeps us living and breathing every single moment (Ezekiel 37:5-6). The Holy Spirit is the one who gives us new life when we are born again (Titus 3:5). The Holy Spirit is the source of our life—every part of it! We are His greatest product.

The Bible is the tool in the hand of the Holy Spirit to nurture us and furnish us with everything we need to succeed on earth (2 Timothy 3:16-17). Jesus used the weapon of the Word, the sword of the Spirit, when Satan tempted Him.

Jesus simply answered with the words of the Holy Spirit (Luke 4:4).

The Holy Spirit wants to breathe victory into us through His Word. He wants His energy to be poured through us. He wants His wisdom deposited in our hearts. He wants His instincts and nature to be evident in us. He wants us to know what He knows. He wants us to feel what He feels. He wants us to see that which He sees. The Bible is the tool He uses. The Bible is a record of the opinions of the Holy Spirit. As we develop an awareness of the Holy Spirit's opinion, our whole world changes. The Word of God, inspired by the Holy Spirit, produces the nature of an overcomer within us. He gives us the power to Man UP and rise to the top. He is the champion connection (2 Timothy 3:15-17).

The Holy Spirit is able to make us overcomers. He empowered Jesus to overcome Satan in the wilderness of temptation (see Matthew 4). The Holy Spirit knows our seasons of testing and the rewards awaiting us. The Holy Spirit knows the weaknesses of our enemy and the weapons we will need to win any battle.

Jesus trusted the Holy Spirit fully, and we can too. Jesus trusted the Holy Spirit to raise Him from the dead (Romans 8:11). Jesus knew that the anointing/presence of the Holy Spirit would enable the disciples to stand against anything. *"But ye shall receive power, after the Holy Ghost is come upon you: and you shall be witnesses unto me"* (Acts 1:8). That's why Jesus was not worried when Peter denied Him three times. When the disciples fled at the crucifixion, Jesus was not hopeless. He knew the Holy Spirit. He knew what the anointing would do within a person's life. His instruction to tarry in the upper room until the Holy Spirit came was sufficient. Jesus was not trying to make the disciples strong. He was trying to make them aware of the Holy Spirit.

When the Holy Spirit becomes our focus, we will know peace through all circumstances. *"Thou will keep him in perfect peace, whose mind is stayed on thee: because he trusts in thee"* (Isaiah 26:3). Practice the presence of the Holy Spirit in your life every day by following the six steps of intimacy I have shared with you. You can overcome through the Holy Spirit. Develop an addiction to the Holy Spirit. Your dependency upon Him is the key to being a champion and developing intimacy with others.

The Sexual Man Knows

God has given us permission to develop intimacy with our spouse and enjoy our sexuality. He invented sex. We can discover how to enjoy it and develop a thrilling, happy, fulfilled marriage. Proverbs 5:18-19 tells us,

> *Let your fountain [your body parts which produce life] be blessed, and rejoice [or ecstatically delight] with the wife of your youth . . . Let her breasts satisfy you at all times, and be ravished [enraptured] always with her love.*

The emphasis on enjoying sex with our covenant spouse (wife of our youth) is for our happiness not our imprisonment. Sex is empowering because it is meant to say to the person with whom you are making love, "You are my covenant partner. You are the only person on this planet that I allow to have this intimacy with me. No one else can minister to me sexually." That makes you and your partner unique to one another. You are empowered to rejoice and satisfy one another and always be intoxicated with one another (and no one else) sexually.

Ephesians 5 verses 31-32 causes us to understand that the properly executed and mutually satisfying sexual union is God's way of getting us to know a great spiritual truth. *"For this cause shall a man leave his father and mother, and shall be joined unto his wife, and they two shall be one flesh. This is a great mystery, but I speak concerning Christ and the church."* This tells us of the greatest story of love and intimacy ever told— of how Jesus gave Himself for us and is intimately involved with us.

Scripture suggests that just as we can *know* the Holy Spirit, so we can *know* our spouse in an intimate way through the physical act of marriage. *Know* is the term used in Scripture to define our relationship to God; it is also the term used to designate the intimate union of husband and wife in covenant. "Adam *knew* Eve" (Genesis 4:1, emphasis added). Mary, speaking of her virginity, said, "How shall this be, seeing I *know not* a man?" (Luke 1:34, emphasis added). Matthew 1:25 tells us that Joseph "knew her not" until after the birth of Christ. Our sexuality offers us the pleasure of *knowing* the one we love and with whom we are in covenant.

You now *know* how to Man UP and cultivate intimacy. I encourage you to Man UP and get to *know* the Holy Spirit. As your relationship with the Holy Spirit grows, so will your intimacy with your wife.

This has been a heavy chapter that is life changing when followed. If you want to take a break before the next chapter and get to *know* your wife, I understand! Enjoy your break, and I'll see you in chapter five.

Chapter 5

The Superman, Part One

I grew up in Waukegan, Illinois, a suburb of Chicago. My high school had about 2,500 students enrolled. During the late 60s, there was a lot of racial tension, and many gangs formed throughout the school. You had to Man UP to survive. An inexperienced young man who did not know how to Man UP likely would join a gang of friends just to feel protected. Some of us had been in enough fights that we had a reputation so almost everybody would leave us alone. I had been beat up enough times by the bullies and survived, so I had somewhat of a reputation.

During my sophomore year, the racial tension and fighting was so bad that we had policemen with police dogs patrolling the school halls. We had surfers, mods, and greaser gangs, as well as others. I was somewhat of a nomad and tried out all the gangs at one time or another. One day, a new kid named Ed began to attend school. He was huge and greasy. Ed soon developed a reputation, and nobody wanted to mess with Big Ed.

One day some buddies came running through the hall yelling, "Cliff, Cliff, guess what? Big Ed has a list with the names of everybody he can beat up, and your name is on his list!"

"What? There is no way that Big Ed can beat me up!" I exclaimed to my fans. I began to storm through the halls looking for Big Ed. We were going to settle this issue quickly. When I found Big Ed with his group of followers, I went up and got in his face. "I understand you have a list with the names of everybody you can beat up on it. They say my name is on your list. There is no way that you can beat me up . . . I will pulverize you!"

Do you know what Big Ed did? No, he did not punch me and start a fight. He did not cuss me out nor challenge me. Big Ed got out his eraser and said, "You're right," and he took my name off his list!

The devil has a list. On his list are the names of everybody he thinks he can beat up. We must learn how to Man UP and make the devil take our name off his list (1 Peter 5:8-9). We must get in his face and proclaim to him in the name of Jesus, "Devil, you cannot have my marriage. Devil, you cannot have my health. Devil, you cannot have my finances. Devil, you cannot have my family. Devil, take my name off your list, and do it now!"

Clark Kent had a secret identity. Behind his mild mannered, *Daily Planet* newspaper reporter guise, he was Superman. When alerted to trouble and the need for a deliverer, Clark would duck into a phone booth, rip off his clothes to reveal his costume, and emerge as Superman. Faster than a speeding bullet, able to leap tall buildings in a single bound, Superman would arrive on the scene and everything would work out. You have a secret identity too. Under your daily manhood guise, you are a superman who can make the devil take your name off his list and flee in terror.

To make the devil follow your command, you must Man UP and develop the Superman reputation. This reputation is built through an intimate relationship with the Holy Spirit in us. The Bible says that *the* greater one, not *a* greater one but THE GREATER ONE, lives in us (1 John 4:4). We simply need to learn how to release the forces of greatness that are within us. Just as Clark Kent had his Superman costume under his street clothes, so too do you have the ultimate superman living inside you. You just need to release the superman in you!

One historic day in our church, Dr. Oral and Evelyn Roberts were to be our guests. Before the service began, Dr. Roberts requested to meet with me alone, in my office. We prayed together and asked the Holy Spirit what He wanted to accomplish during the service that was about to begin. An awesome presence filled the office as we prayed. I knew we were about to have a memorable service. As we left the office to join Evelyn and Darlene and go into the service, Dr. Roberts told me he was to sow a seed today and asked me not to receive an offering for his ministry. I humbly agreed.

During the service, Dr. Roberts received an offering for our ministry. It was the largest single offering we had ever received. Dr. Roberts did not know that in our twenty year ministry we had never owned our own property. We were leasing our current building and believing God to one day become property owners and own the campus we were renting. The offering Dr. Roberts received enabled us to begin the process to purchase the church and campus. In a matter of months, despite some tough negotiations, we supernaturally became the owners of the multimillion dollar campus.

Dr. Oral Roberts was a superman to me. He was a man who knew how to Man UP. He was supernaturally endowed to birth miracles. He was a man who, through his relationship with the Holy Spirit, helped turn impossibilities into possibilities.

Jesus Christ is the ultimate Superman. He enables you to become a superman too and turn impossibilities into possibilities. Jesus takes great delight in taking us from zero to hero and making us supermen. How does this happen? How can we become supermen? The answer is found in the story of Jesus' birth.

How Superman Mans UP

Mary was going about her daily routine, taking care of business as usual. Suddenly with no warning or time to prepare, God interrupted her day. An angel appeared and told Mary that she was favored by God and would conceive the Christ. Of course, Mary was overwhelmed with this announcement. She courageously embraced the message from God and said, "Be it done unto me according to the word of the Lord" (Luke 1:34-37).

Mary then asked the obvious question. "How can this happen? I am a virgin. How can I have a child?"

Mary was not challenging the word of the Lord; she was simply inquiring how the seemingly impossible could happen. She knew it would require a supernatural miracle. How could it be? That is a question all of us ask at some time in our manhood. How can I be a superman? Sometimes I feel as though I can barely exist as a man. How can I become a hero? How can I make the devil take my name off his list? How can I become a solution for someone else?

The answer the angel gave to Mary's question is the same answer for you and me. The angel said, "The Holy Spirit will overshadow you; that is how this will happen." How will you become a superman? The Holy Spirit will overshadow you. How will you become a hero? The Holy Spirit will overshadow you. How will you be a solution for the problems you are facing? The Holy Spirit will overshadow you. How will you Man UP and become a superman? The Holy Spirit will overshadow you!

Real men want to be more than average or mediocre. Wise men realize we need help to rise above mediocrity to live an overcoming life. If we don't need any help, if we have life figured out and we have it all together, then why did Jesus say He would send us a Helper (John 16:7)? The promise of a helper presupposes that we need help. This was Jesus' way of tipping us off to one of the most profound truths: leading a victorious life is impossible without a helper. You cannot be a superman without a supernatural helper.

Superman's Secret

How does the Holy Spirit help us to be supermen? He lives inside those who have accepted Jesus Christ as their personal Savior. His presence in us is the potential for becoming a superman. In addition to living inside believers, the Holy Spirit longs to come upon individuals and release His anointing upon them. This enables us to perform as a superman.

Let's look at these two functions of the Holy Spirit to understand how they work. We Man UP and become a superman when these two functions—the Holy Spirit in us and the Holy Spirit upon us—are working together. The Holy Spirit in us is like Clark Kent with his Superman identity hidden. The Holy Spirit upon us is like Clark Kent stepping out of the phone booth as Superman for all to see.

Let me share how these two functions of the Holy Spirit make us supermen. There are different theories concerning the indwelling of the Holy Spirit in believers. Some say the Holy Spirit indwells believers at the moment of salvation. Others say that the Holy Spirit indwells believers sometime after they believe. I want to focus on the one fact upon which we all agree—however and whenever it happens, the Holy Spirit indwells the believer (1 Corinthians 3:16). This is the first secret to becoming a superman.

In addition to the Holy Spirit indwelling man, we need to understand another function of the Holy Spirit that makes us supermen (it takes both functions working together). In addition to the Holy Spirit in man, we must understand the Holy Spirit coming upon us and releasing His anointing— the superman empowering.

Before we can operate as a superman, we need to understand that the Holy Spirit has a mind and will of His own. The Holy Spirit makes decisions. The Holy Spirit is not a power that can be harnessed or manipulated. To be overshadowed by the Holy Spirit is not to enhance our own ability to carry out our own will. On the contrary, the power of the Holy Spirit is available only to those who intend to carry out His will. He is not our servant. He is our guide and helper (1 Corinthians 2:11-12; 12:11).

The Holy Spirit is a gift and the giver of gifts. The Holy Spirit places seeds of greatness in each of us (Luke 11:13; 1 Corinthians 12:4-11). The Holy Spirit expects us to develop and grow the gift(s) He gives to us. We can Man UP and become supermen through intimacy with the Holy Spirit (Matthew 11:11; 1 John 4:4). Nobody else has the total knowledge of all our gifts and talents like the Holy Spirit does. As we cultivate intimacy with the Holy Spirit in us, we will discover that He also comes upon us and enables us to arise from mediocrity to greatness.

Jesus Trusted the Holy Spirit

The Holy Spirit is also called the Spirit of Christ (Romans 8:9). Jesus trusted the Holy Spirit fully, and we can too. Jesus trusted the Holy Spirit to raise Him from the dead. That's one of the reasons He was willing to go through Calvary (Romans 8:11).

Jesus knew that the Holy Spirit would enable the disciples to Man UP and be supermen who could stand against anything. That's why Jesus was not worried when Peter denied Him three times. When the disciples fled at the crucifixion, Jesus was not hopeless. He knew the Holy Spirit. He knew what the Holy Spirit in a person's life would do. His instruction for the apostles to tarry in the upper room until the Holy Spirit came was sufficient. Jesus was not trying to make the disciples strong. He was trying to make them aware of the Holy Spirit who would empower them.

The Holy Spirit will remind us of the principles of Jesus Christ and the mandates that we have previously heard (John 14:26). The Word of God, inspired by the Holy Spirit, produces the nature of superman (overcomer) within us (2 Timothy 3:15-17).

The Holy Spirit enables us to Man UP and become a superman/overcomer. He empowered Jesus to overcome

Satan in the wilderness of temptation. The Holy Spirit knows the seasons of our testing and rewards. He knows the weaknesses of our enemies and the weapons we need to win any battle (Acts 10:38).

When the Holy Spirit becomes our focus, we will have confidence in our ability to be supermen. We will have peace through all circumstances (Isaiah 26:3). We can overcome any bad habit, inner grief, or chaotic situation through the Holy Spirit. We need to practice the presence of the Holy Spirit within us every day and develop an addiction to Him. We cultivate an intimacy with Him through prayer, Bible study, and praise and worship.

The Holy Spirit knows the thoughts of God. He imparts wisdom to believers in Jesus Christ and conforms us to His image. An intimate relationship with the Holy Spirit is the key to understanding the wisdom of God. The Holy Spirit will tell us what to say, when to say it, what to do, when to do it, and even reveal the future to us. Then He will come upon us and give us the supernatural ability to accomplish the assignment. The Holy Spirit wants to make us a superman!

During a break in a Christmas play rehearsal, a young boy came running up to the pastor and announced, "I'm a wise man!"

"You are?" said the pastor. "You seem pretty excited about it."

The boy exclaimed, "I am!"

"What's so great about being a wise man?" the pastor asked.

The boy quickly replied, "I get to carry the gold . . . and I don't have to hang around any smelly ol' sheep."

Many men in our world today seem to have a similar view of wisdom. They believe wisdom is the ability to "carry the gold"—to make a good living, to live a comfortable life, and to avoid association with anything unpleasant.

God's Word points us to a different definition of wisdom: the capacity to see things from God's perspective and to respond to them according to scriptural principles. God wants us to walk wisely so that we may be entrusted with superman ability. God desires that we avoid the strength draining kryptonite associated with foolish living.

We face challenging decisions every day. Some decisions involve our health, our work, our finances, and our families. Each of these areas tends to change over time. We continually find ourselves facing new circumstances. To acquire godly wisdom, we must consciously and intentionally ask the Holy Spirit to reveal His wisdom in the midst of every challenge (James 1:5-8).

There are only two ways to live in this life—wisely or unwisely. The man who chooses to Man UP chooses wisely and experiences God's presence and power. Wisdom is not difficult to find. Proverbs tells us that wisdom calls out loud and raises her voice to be heard. We must be diligent in our pursuit of wisdom.

Lady Wisdom and Superman

I wondered why wisdom is always referred to as "she" in the Scriptures and not as a "he." I asked the Holy Spirit about this and heard the following explanation: the Holy Spirit said, "Wisdom is she because just as a woman responds to you according to how you treat her, so wisdom responds to you according to how you treat her."

Proverbs 4:5 tells us to get wisdom and get understanding. The two are not the same. Understanding tells us *what* is happening. Wisdom tells us *why* it is happening. Understanding gives us the facts. Wisdom tells us what to do with those facts. Wisdom tells us which solution to pursue, and when and how to pursue it. Scripture tells us we must get both wisdom and understanding. Many people have understanding. Wisdom only comes through intimacy with the Spirit of wisdom, the Holy Spirit. It takes a man of courage to cultivate intimacy with the Holy Spirit. Through this process, we are enabled with wisdom and power that makes us a superman!

How will you become a superman? How will you release the champion in you? How will you accomplish supernatural results when you perform as the leading man in the drama of life? You need to Man UP and partner with the Holy Spirit. Drawing power from the Holy Spirit and utilizing His wisdom is how you will accomplish supernatural results. The Holy Spirit is the champion in you.

When evil, adversity, or danger was rampant, Clark Kent would have to duck into a phone booth or a closet and rip off his average man disguise to reveal his true Superman identity. Your true identity is a superman.

In the next chapter, we will discover how to reveal and release the champion in us.

Chapter 6

The Superman, Part Two

Perhaps you heard about the man who desperately wanted to be a superman. He decided to bless his wife with a new refrigerator. He purchased the model with all the bells and whistles and paid nearly three thousand dollars for it. He arranged for the refrigerator to be delivered that afternoon.

On his way home, he was so excited he decided to stop at the grocery store and purchase all the goodies the family loved that could go into the new refrigerator. He picked out the family's favorite ice cream, fresh vegetables, sodas, fruit, cake, and steaks—everything they all enjoyed.

The refrigerator arrived at home that evening, and his wife loved it. She was joyful to stock it with the goodies and looked forward to being able to serve her family wonderful meals.

The family went to bed after a great evening together. The next morning when the husband awakened, he went into the kitchen to admire his newest acquisition. He was shocked! Melted ice cream was all over the floor. The milk was sour, and the meat was warm and already smelling up the kitchen. It was evident that his brand new, top-of-the-line refrigerator was not working.

Angry and disgusted, he called the manager of the store where he purchased the refrigerator to give them a piece of his mind for selling him a dud. The salesperson who handled the deal was surprised at the news. She asked him to pull open the freezer door to see if the light turned on. He did so, but no light came on. She then asked him to put his ear to the bottom of the refrigerator to see if he heard the low hum of the motor. He did so, but there was no noise. Finally, she asked him to look behind the refrigerator and see if the electrical cord had been plugged in the outlet. He did so and to his surprise found that the cord was lying on the floor unplugged! He returned to the phone to inform the saleslady that the refrigerator was unplugged, but that shouldn't matter. He argued that for several thousand dollars, the appliance should work—plugged in or not! (Some of us are pretty stubborn and don't want to admit our mistakes.)

The saleslady then explained a very important secret to the man: namely, refrigerators are dependent electrical appliances—they were never made to work on their own. They are built with certain specifications that can only work when they are connected to electrical power. While all the necessary parts are there, the refrigerator will not accomplish its purpose until it is connected to the power source to which it was created to be connected.

As men, we must stay connected to our power source, the Holy Spirit! Jesus said that apart from Him, we can do nothing (John 15:4-5). We must Man UP and stay connected to the Holy Spirit to operate as supermen.

Man UP or Man DOWN

I read about a well-known old man who did not know how to Man UP and stay connected to the Holy Spirit, so he became a man down! His home was a mess of cardboard boxes and trash stashed under a freeway bridge. His transportation was a rusty grocery cart with wobbly wheels.

During the hot Texas summer, he would panhandle for change from drivers who were stopped at the intersection. In the winter, it was easier to go through the trash dumpsters behind the hotels for food scraps.

One fierce winter day, he didn't make his usual rounds. At first, no one noticed. If they had noticed, it wouldn't have mattered because it was too miserable outside to go looking for an old man. Two days later, someone found him. He had wasted away with pneumonia and died in his cold, cardboard home, covered with old newspapers for warmth.

When an autopsy was done, they found a safe-deposit box key tightly clasped in the old man's right hand. At first, it was thought the old man had just found the key on the street or had stolen it. An investigation revealed, however, that the deposit box had been issued in the old man's name years ago.

What the lawyers found in the box when they opened it was the deed to the old man's mansion in Florida that was unoccupied for years. There were stocks and bonds that were untouched for years. They found a diploma from Harvard, a Rolex watch, stacks of $100 bills, small plastic containers filled with gold coins, and a diamond ring valued at several thousand dollars.

The old man who had lived in such misery and lack was, in reality, a very wealthy man. He possessed incredible resources but did not use them. He was legally connected to all he needed for a comfortable life, but for unknown reasons never enjoyed what he had.

This is a picture of too many men. To Man UP or to Man DOWN is our choice. If we make no choice, that in reality is a choice. It is the choice not to choose, but it is a choice. As believers in Jesus Christ, we have the power of God available for us to live a victorious life (John 10:10). We have been made kings and priests and have been blessed with every spiritual blessing (Revelation 1:6; Eph. 1:3). We have been given authority over all the forces of the enemy and have the omnipotent power of God available to us (Luke 10:19; Ephesians 1:19-20). But we must choose to connect with what is available.

Superman Power

The Apostle Paul talked about being able to live as more than a mere man. He talked about being able to live as a superman (2 Peter 1:4; 1 Corinthians 3:3). To be empowered to live as supermen, we must cultivate intimacy with the person of the Holy Spirit. He will empower us to overcome any adversary or evil that lurks. Not even kryptonite can stop the Holy Spirit-empowered superman.

My life dramatically changed when I met the Holy Spirit as a person. I learned how to connect to the power of manhood through intimacy with Him. I want to share the secret of this connection with you. The Holy Spirit is more than a presence or a force. He is a person.

You may ask, "How can you know a person you cannot see?" A relationship between any two people involves mutual interaction. They communicate with each other and experience each other. Jesus trusted the Holy Spirit fully, and we can too. Jesus trusted the Holy Spirit to raise Him from the dead. That's one of the reasons He was willing to go through Calvary (Romans 8:11). Jesus had learned to communicate with the Holy Spirit.

I have always admired and studied Abraham Lincoln. If I wanted to have a relationship with him, I could study his life to learn what he was like. I could visit his tomb and read his writings and books about him so I could gain an appreciation for the kind of person he was. But I still would not have communicated with Abraham Lincoln.

Relationship requires interaction. Abe could never talk to me or acknowledge my presence. Without the ability to communicate with Abraham Lincoln, I can never have a true relationship (connection) with him. I may know about him, but I can never know him.

Many men know *about* the Holy Spirit. Many men have the Holy Spirit living in them but still do not know how to communicate (connect) with Him. The people in the Bible who are examples of how to Man UP and be supernaturally empowered were people who actually communicated with God. They didn't just know *about* God, they interacted *with* Him. Interaction and intimacy with the Spirit of the living God is how we Man UP.

I'd like to share a true Superman experience I read once about a politician named Dan. This man enjoyed walking alone or with his new friends along the river. Though he was far from home, separated from his old friends and family, there was something about the quiet water of the great river that gave him a peaceful feeling. Sometimes he would walk alone for hours, praying and meditating on the Scriptures.

As he walked along the beautiful green river bank with some friends one day, however, something unusual happened. Several men from the government office where he worked had joined him for an afternoon stroll. As they walked together, they chatted about the affairs of state, the political climate, and the threat of war.

As they neared the bend of the river on the outskirts of the city, Dan felt a strange physical sensation. The air seemed to thicken. He felt weak and found himself struggling for a breath. His whole body began to tremble as he felt waves of heat rolling over him.

At first he thought he might be coming down with the flu, but it was clear that the men with him were experiencing the same sensations. His associates exchanged terrified glances and cried out, "What is this? I'm getting out of here!" In their fear, in a somewhat comical display, they turned and fled through the mud into the tall reeds beside the river.

In the midst of the phenomenon, however, Dan felt no need to flee; instead, he felt a strange sense of peace. After the initial surprise, he sensed the familiar presence of the Holy Spirit around him. He began to feel weaker, and his knees trembled.

Looking up, he saw what appeared to be a golden light speaking to him. He was able to make out that it was an angel. Before he could hear what the angel was saying, he was overwhelmed by the mighty presence of God. His face turned pale, and he fell to the ground, unconscious.

How did you respond to the true story you just read? Did it seem strange and make you a little skeptical? Maybe you thought it was a little weird. Or maybe you have had a similar experience to which you can relate. You may have recognized that Dan's experience is found in Daniel 10 in the Bible. It was a real encounter with God (Daniel 10:4-11).

Daniel's experience with God included physiological responses. These types of responses should not be feared but need to be understood. You may experience some similar responses when you Man UP and the Holy Spirit comes upon you and empowers you to be a superman.

Man UP with the Holy Spirit

Okay, so how do we get plugged in and stay connected to the Holy Spirit? How do we Man UP and become empowered and overshadowed to live as supermen? We begin by confronting any fear about intimacy with the Holy Spirit. We need to understand that the Holy Spirit desires to indwell us as men to enable us to grow His fruit in our character. When He indwells us, He enables us to understand the Scriptures so we can live by the principles therein and receive the wisdom necessary for successful manhood. Secondly, we need to expect the Holy Spirit to come upon us at times as He did Daniel and empower us to accomplish His destiny for us as men.

To truly experience and connect with the Holy Spirit, we must understand the twofold desire that the Holy Spirit has for man:

• to live in (indwell) man and
• to come upon (anoint/empower) man.

These are two separate works of the Holy Spirit with man. Both are necessary for us to perform as a superman.

The first thing the Holy Spirit does in us when He lives in (indwells) us is to bring us into a new understanding of the

Bible. He illumines the Word. With our new understanding of the Word, we learn how to live successfully in the world. As we obey the revelation of the Scriptures, we will become conformed to the image of Jesus Christ. The Bible, once a dry book, will read as an exciting Book filled with life (John 16:13-14). The indwelling Spirit will be a well of living water for He leads us into all truth and reveals the things of Jesus to us (John 14-16).

When the Holy Spirit lives in us, we are able to understand true love and bear the fruit of the Spirit. It is the Holy Spirit who sheds the love of God in our hearts and places the desires of Jesus' heart into us (Romans 5:5).

The indwelling ministry of the Holy Spirit begins at the moment of salvation. The indwelling is not usually experiential. That is, when the Holy Spirit comes into us, there is not usually any discernible feeling associated with it. We receive Him by faith, and He begins His work in our lives.

We begin to change when the Holy Spirit indwells us, and His fruit becomes more and more evident in our lives. The fruit of the Spirit is not something we have to strain to produce. A fruit tree doesn't have to struggle and strive to bear fruit; it just grows. As we grow in our manhood, filled with the Holy Spirit, we discover that it is easier to love than it used to be. We tend to be more joyful and discover greater peace in our hearts and minds (Galatians 5:16-26).

The Empowering

The Holy Spirit also desires to empower us to accomplish His destiny for our lives (1 Corinthians 2:4-5). The empowering of the Holy Spirit is what happened to Daniel in our preceding story. It is an experience that equips people with supernatural resources to accomplish the work of God (John 14:12). This empowering has been called by many names such as the "baptism of the Holy Spirit" or "being filled by the Spirit" or "the anointing." It is frequently referred to in Scripture as the Spirit "coming upon" or "being poured out on" or simply "being on" a person (Matthew 3:11; Acts 2:4,33; 1:8). This empowering happened to men throughout the Old Testament (before the Holy Spirit indwelled man) as well as in the New Testament (Judges 3:9-11; 1 Samuel 10:1-11; Daniel 10:4-11).

In Old Testament times, the ministry of the Holy Spirit "upon" people was limited. Only a chosen few were allowed this experience. But God promised a time would come when the empowering work of the Holy Spirit would be available to all (Joel 2:28-29). In Peter's sermon on the day of Pentecost, he said that the time spoken of by Joel had arrived (Acts 2:16-18). The empowering of the Holy Spirit is now available to all of God's people.

Observable Evidence

The empowering of the Holy Spirit is an experience of the Holy Spirit coming upon us. It is evident something has happened to us. When Philip preached in Samaria, many people were born again. However, Scripture states that it was obvious the Holy Spirit had not come upon any of them. This indicates that there were outward signs Philip looked for to determine if a person had received the Holy Spirit's empowering (Acts 8:16). (Some have referred to these evidences as the Superman costume. They are the outward physical displays of the superman inside man.)

Peter and John arrived in Samaria, laid hands on the people, and something happened. There was an observable experience of the Holy Spirit coming upon the people (Acts 8:18-19). This experience was so observable and dramatic that a magician offered Peter and John money to teach him how to anoint people like that.

The work of maturing that comes to man through the indwelling ministry of the Holy Spirit comes through a gradual process (1 Peter 3:18; Romans 5:4). The empowering or coming upon man is usually a sudden outpouring where we are drenched with His power. It's like going to the ocean and having a big wave crash down on you. Many times the evidence of this coming upon man by the Holy Spirit is a release of a spiritual gift. Frequently, the empowering is accompanied by a gift such as speaking in tongues or prophesying (Acts 2; 10:45-46; 19:5-6).

Others have shared that a sensation of heat came upon them. Some have felt waves of power or unexplainable weeping or laughing. As we saw in Daniel's experience, there are many biblical evidences of the Holy Spirit coming upon a person.

It is not wrong to seek an experience with the Holy Spirit. We are told to desire earnestly the gifts and power of God (1 Corinthians 12-14). The Apostle Paul always yearned for more power (Philippians 3:10).

Superman Communicates

The Holy Spirit is the master communicator. The Holy Spirit talks more than anybody I know. He knows everybody. He can speak every language and can talk to people everywhere at the same time. He can speak to thousands simultaneously. The cry of Jesus for us today is, *"He that has an ear, let him hear, what the Spirit says"* (Revelation 2:7, 11, 17).

When the Holy Spirit fills our lives, our manner of speaking may change immediately because our hearts have been changed. Beyond that, however, speaking in tongues is also an evidence of the Holy Spirit. I believe that all Christians may pray in tongues and interpret. First Corinthians 14 tells us not to forbid tongues because when we pray in tongues, we speak to God and not to man and thereby edify ourselves. Jesus said, *"These signs will follow he who believes in me: In my name they will cast out demons; they will speak with new tongues"* (Mark 16:17).

While speaking in tongues is available to all believers, to insist that tongues is the *only* evidence of the baptism of the Holy Spirit seems improper and invalidates the experience of all those saints whose lives have given abundant evidence of being lived in the power of the Holy Spirit but who have never spoken in tongues.

The pursuit of love is the goal of Christians. To possess any gift without the fruit or love of the Spirit is useless. The fruit of the Spirit makes it possible for the Christian to exercise the gifts of the Spirit in a manner that would bring glory to God. Christians should be known by their fruit rather than by their gifts. The most visible evidence of the Spirit-filled life should be a brand new love—love for God, the brethren, and a lost world.

It should be remembered that the empowering of the Holy Spirit is not a once and for all event. We need subsequent times of anointing. To Man UP is to be filled and refilled throughout life. The disciples were filled with God's power in Acts 2, but then they prayed again and were filled again in Acts 4. Paul tells us in Ephesians to keep on being filled with the Holy Spirit.

The purpose of the Holy Spirit upon man is to equip us to minister to others and to change lives through the power of God (Acts 1:8). These experiences of empowering are difficult to describe but are very real. Throughout history, there have been many views about the Holy Spirit and His role in man. I do not want to create a dogma about the Holy Spirit indwelling man and the Holy Spirit coming upon man. I simply want to make you aware that the Holy Spirit is a real person who wants to equip you to be a superman.

The Superman Criteria

It is important to understand that not everyone experiences the Holy Spirit the same way. It is also necessary to understand that if you have never had an experience with the Holy Spirit the way Daniel and others did, you are still blessed! Read the words of Jesus when He was talking about one of His disciples who wanted a visible, physical experience in order to believe in the resurrection.

Now Thomas, called the Twin, one of the twelve, was not with them when Jesus came. The other disciples therefore said to him, "We have seen the Lord." So he said to them, "Unless I see in His hands the print of the nails, and put my finger into the print of the nails, and put my hand into His side, I will not believe." And after eight days His disciples were again inside, and Thomas with them. Jesus came, the doors being shut, and stood in the midst, and said, "Peace to you!" Then He said to Thomas, "Reach your finger here, and look at my hands; and reach your hand here, and put it into my side. Do not be unbelieving, but believing." And Thomas answered and said to Him, "My Lord and my God!" Jesus said to him, "Thomas, because you have seen me, you have believed. Blessed are those who have not seen and yet have believed."

And truly Jesus did many other signs in the presence of His disciples, which are not written in this book; but these are written that you may believe that Jesus is the Christ, the Son of God, and that believing you may have life in His name (John 20:24-30).

Jesus performs many signs and wonders even today. Many have testified of wonderful experiences that have changed their lives. Others have not had an experience with the Holy Spirit as the one Daniel had. Jesus wanted to let us know that believing in Him, not having supernatural experiences is the criteria for being blessed. As we have discussed, it is not wrong to desire supernatural experiences, but it would be wrong to consider ourselves more or less spiritual because we did or did not have such an experience. We must keep on believing in Christ and cultivating intimacy with His Holy Spirit. The Holy Spirit will reveal Himself to us as He wills. Through the journey of cultivating intimacy with the Holy Spirit, His power and presence will be evident in your life.

A tale from India of four blind men who heard of a fantastic creature called an elephant helps put the many facets of the Holy Spirit into perspective.

Determined to learn more about the strange creature, the blind men arranged to go and experience the elephant for themselves. Entering the village where the elephant was kept, the blind men groped until they encountered the beast.

The first man bumped against the elephant's side. He carefully ran his hands up and down, then back and forth along the dusty hide of the elephant. This man announced to everyone within hearing distance, "I see what an elephant is like! An elephant is like a wall!"

The second blind man encountered the elephant's leg. Feeling the leg in his nervous hands, he answered back, "What are you talking about? An elephant is not like a wall. An elephant is like a tree!"

The third blind man ran into the elephant's tusk. He felt its hard, sharply pointed tip. He rebuked his friends. "What foolishness is this? You are both crazy. An elephant is nothing like a wall or a tree. I can tell you from experience that an elephant is like a spear!"

The fourth blind man reached and found the elephant's powerful trunk. Jumping back in terror, he shouted, "You are all wrong! I know for a fact that an elephant is like a great snake!"

The four blind men left the village in a clamorous argument about the true nature of an elephant. Each was thoroughly convinced that he was right and the others were wrong. Each based his judgment on his own personal experience, never suspecting that there was far more to an elephant that what any of them could comprehend.

My prayer is that you will fear God, believe in Jesus Christ, and receive the Holy Spirit to live in you. To Man UP is to cultivate this relationship with the Holy Spirit. Our experiences may be different, but our Lord and Savior is the same Jesus Christ! Let's grow in love as we Man UP and become real supermen.

Chapter 7

The Fireman

Every man dreams of being a hero. It wasn't always the case, but after 9/11, firemen are recognized as real heroes and rightly so. Firemen must Man UP and face danger in order to save lives. To become a hero, we must have overcome some adversity and helped others to overcome and avoid disaster. When we Man UP, we can qualify as firemen who know how to overcome the fires of adversity. We will be true heroes as we overcome adversity and help others to discover purpose and fulfillment in life. Let's look at three young men who were genuine firemen that became real heroes. Their exhilarating story is found in the Bible in the book of Daniel.

King Nebuchadnezzar had commissioned the royal artisans to make a golden image of himself, and he established a national holiday for all the people so they could come and worship him. He issued invitations on palace stationery, inviting all the bigwigs in the land to come to his party and advertised on all the local channels that he was throwing this huge fireman's ball.

Actually, he didn't "invite" anyone; he commanded

everyone to come. It was a royal edict that everyone had to come to the plain of Dura and bow down in homage before this huge golden statue of him. The alternative to bowing before the statue was simple: death by fire. Since most of his people were terrified of him, they hurried to obey.

So "everybody who is anybody" came, attired in his or her dress uniforms or finest silk gowns, and they all mingled at this huge cocktail party at the royal palace. Then, when the orchestra struck up the new national anthem, "Hail Nebuchadnezzar the Terrible," everybody bowed down low before the statue and worshipped King Nebuchadnezzar as a god.

Everybody also groveled out on the plain of Dura, chanting, "Hail to thee, O great god Nebuchadnezzar! Live long and prosper, O awesome king! We worship thee, our god of gold!" Everyone worshipped . . . except three young Jewish men named Shadrach, Meshach, and Abednego. They wouldn't put their fear of man ahead of their obedience to God. (My aunt used to say their names as "shake the bed, make the bed, and in the bed we go.")

These three courageous men refused to bow down to the king. They chose to Man UP and be firemen (remember, they had a death-by-fire sentence hanging over their heads). When the very angry king heard about their refusal—for of course, it was immediately brought to his attention by some self-seeking sycophants—he demanded, "If your choices are either to worship the idol or to be thrown into the furnace of blazing fire, why do you refuse to obey?"

The three boys calmly answered, "Our God whom we serve is able to deliver us from the furnace, and He will deliver us out of your hand." Shadrach, Meshach, and

Abednego believed that God was a fireman and would deliver them. They went on to say that even if God did not deliver them, they would not bow the knee to any other God. WOW! This would be some fireman's ball!

The Fury of the King

Their answer enraged Nebuchadnezzar even more. The Bible says, "The expression on his face changed toward Shadrach, Meshach, and Abednego." For humble Jewish boys to be talking face-to-face with the mighty king was a protocol breaking situation. But because it was his specially declared holiday, Nebuchadnezzar was feeling magnanimous. Actually, he did his best to give them the benefit of the doubt. However, since they didn't grovel and snivel like all the rest of the governors, administrators, and officials but answered him in a straightforward, uncompromising, non-defensive manner, this lit the king's temper like the fuse on a firecracker.

Furiously, he ordered that the furnace be heated up seven times hotter than ever before. He was known for his tough "justice" and wanted to be completely sure to eradicate these rebels before they could influence the rest of his people. Then he called on the strongest warriors in his kingdom—the biggest, most-decorated, best-renowned soldiers that he had—to tie up the three firemen and throw them into the furnace. When these elite warriors tried to get close to the blazing furnace, they themselves were overcome by the tremendous heat. However, finally someone managed to get the boys at least close enough to topple them into the furnace; and Shadrach, Meshach, and Abednego fell inside the fire, all tied up.

The Ultimate Fireman

When the king looked into the furnace to watch the helpless boys being burned to death, he saw not three but four figures! The boys were not tied up any longer either; in fact, they were peacefully walking around inside the fire! Who were these four brave firemen?

Nebuchadnezzar asked his courtiers, "Didn't we just throw in three people? But I see four men! And that fourth guy—wow! He is something else! He looks like . . . like the Son of God!" Surprise! It was Jesus, the ultimate fireman! He came to rescue the boys who had decided to Man UP.

When did the ultimate fireman show up in the fire with Shadrach, Meshach, and Abednego? When they were accused and humiliated? No. When they were tried and sentenced to an awful execution? No. When they were tied up by the king's soldiers? No. When they were picked up and thrown into the awful furnace? No. Once they were inside the middle of the fiery furnace, that's when the ultimate fireman arrived! When the circumstances went from lousy to bad to worse, they chose to Man UP, and their faith never wavered. They knew that God would protect them because He was with them. They had courage. To be a fireman that overcomes the fiercest of the fires of adversity, we must take courage and know God is with us.

When you Man UP and go through the fire, it does not have to have any power over you. Your hair won't be singed, your clothes won't be burned, and you won't even smell like smoke.

The satraps, administrators, governors, and the king's counselors gathered together, and they saw these men on whose bodies the fire had no power; the hair of their head was not singed nor were their garments affected, and the smell of fire was not on them (Daniel 3:27).

That's the kind of protection I like over my body and soul, over my possessions, and over my reputation. When calamity comes near me, I need to take courage and know that God is with me! I need to know that God, the ultimate fireman, is with me enabling me to overcome. I need to Man UP and trust God.

When Nebuchadnezzar released the firemen from the fire, the three boys had become true heroes. The king said, *"Blessed be the God of Shadrach, Meshach, and Abednego, who sent His Angel [fireman] and delivered His servants who trusted in Him"* (Daniel 3:28). Notice that the king said, the God of Shadrach, Meshach and Abednego is *the* God. He didn't say He was "the God of the cosmos" or "the God of the universe," not even "the God of Israel." He knew the fireman God as "the God of Shadrach, Meshach, and Abednego." What a testimony! The world today will know God as your God, not the God of the cosmos, nor the God of the church, but as *your* God when you Man UP and pass through the fires of adversity.

Fire Precedes Promotion

All fire precedes promotion. Scripture says, *"Then the king promoted Shadrach, Meshach and Abednego, in the province of Babylon"* (Daniel 3:30). Remember, when you pass through the fire that there is a completion date scheduled for your journey. It is a place of passage, not a place of permanence

(Isaiah 43:1-3). Remember that fire precedes promotion. When you finish your journey through the fire, God guarantees to promote you!

It takes wisdom and training to become an effective fireman. Firemen are trained by learning skills through putting out real fires. Adversity may appear to be an obstacle to you. But God will use it to make you into a hero. Don't run from the battle. Take courage from God. Begin to praise and worship God, and He will join you in the fires of adversity and enable you to come out of the fire and not even smell like smoke.

The Bible tells us that the fear of the Lord is the beginning of wisdom. Therefore, we cannot get wisdom unless we are living in the fear of the Lord (Proverbs 1:7). We are living in the fear of the Lord when we have decided to put away childish things and Man UP. We can then acquire God's wisdom that will enable us to overcome any fires of adversity. Living in the fear of the Lord is how we become firemen.

In the Bible, the real life story of Joseph is another example of becoming a hero through overcoming the fires of adversity. Joseph was betrayed by his brothers and sold as a slave. He was falsely accused of sexual harassment and rape, and imprisoned. To make matters worse, Joseph was kept in prison long after he should have been released. Yet through all of this, he was able to Man UP. Joseph emerged as a winner and became a hero.

Through it all, Joseph never once murmured or complained. Joseph knew the secret of enjoying favor with God and man, and this favor was the secret to his success. Everything Joseph touched prospered. He knew how to find God's favor by living in the fear of the Lord.

The fear of the Lord is to respect the Lord and choose

His ways. *"When a man's ways please the Lord, He makes even his enemies to be at peace with him"* (Proverbs 16:7). When our ways please God, then God will make our enemies be at peace with us. They may not want to be at peace with us, but they will be made so by God. They may remain enemies, but they will have to watch as we enjoy God's banquet table of blessings in their presence (Psalm 23:5). However, we cannot overlook the condition of these blessings: our ways must please God! When our ways please God, no adversity can overtake us, and we are fireproof. We have learned to Man UP.

God gives favor. It is a spiritual force that we must find and operate to maintain true manhood. Without the ingredient of God's favor, there is little we can accomplish. Joseph could achieve accomplishments through adversity because he had found God's favor.

What ultimately happened to Joseph? Joseph went from honored son to dishonored brother, to slave, to comptroller of a rich man's household, to prisoner, to prime minister of the land. His life was a series of the fires of adversity, yet his unswerving faith in God and his willingness to live in the fear of the Lord brought him great reward. He found favor in the sight of God and man. When we choose to Man UP as Joseph did, we will know God's favor in our lives.

Evidence of Favor

How do we find God's favor? First, let us determine the evidence of having God's favor in our lives. Psalm 41:11 tells us that God's favor guarantees no adversity can overcome us! Please note that God never said we wouldn't have enemies, we wouldn't have adversity, or that we wouldn't have problems in our lives; but He did promise that we would not be overcome by them!

God is no respecter of persons in terms of His love for mankind and His standard of judging mankind (see Romans 2:11). God loves us equally, and we will all be judged by the same standard without respect of achievement. However, we can find God's favor and become fireproof. When our ways please God, even our enemies must be at peace with us.

How To Find Favor

How did Joseph find God's favor? How do we find God's favor? The answer is simple: we must walk in the fear of the Lord. The Bible says that the fear of the Lord is to hate evil (Proverbs 8:13). The Bible also says that the fear of the Lord is the beginning of wisdom (Proverbs 9:10). So wisdom only comes to man in proportion to our hatred of evil.

If you walked into your living room and there was a huge pile of cow manure on your floor, you are going to have one of two possible reactions: you will immediately get a shovel and begin to remove the mess, or you will just leave your living room because you don't want to be around fresh cow manure!

Let the manure represent evil or sin. Some people pray, "Oh God, keep me from sin! Don't give me more than I can handle!" And then they walk right into the manure pile. Splat. Ugh! They don't get a shovel and remove it. They don't leave the room. They just pray, "Oh God, please help me," and stay in the middle of the manure. That's ignorance! They have absolutely no concept of the fear of the Lord. Most people do wrong because they don't know how to do right! They would do right if they knew how.

Consider, for example, a beautiful sixteen-year-old girl who loves her mom and dad with all her heart. She would do nothing to embarrass or hurt her parents. She is naïve and has never been taught how to protect herself. If a boy gets her into a parked car and knows how to take advantage of a sexually naïve girl, all the love in her heart for her parents will not protect her. She must have knowledge of where to kick that dog! She must know how to say no, how to scream, and how to avoid the situation before it gets dangerous. Her love for Mom and Dad is not an issue—her knowledge is the issue!

I would never challenge your love for Jesus, but I must challenge your knowledge. God said that without knowledge, His children are destroyed (Hosea 4:6). They are not destroyed by a lack of love, or by a lack of resources, but by a lack of knowledge.

The Secret of the Lord

We don't have the ability to be fireproof if we do not fear the Lord. God loves us whether or not we fear Him. However, His blessing and favor only goes to those who walk in the fear of the Lord.

Let me highlight for you some of the blessings and rewards firemen receive for walking in the fear of the Lord:

Blessed family, wealth, and riches: *"How blessed is the man who fears the Lord . . . his descendants will be mighty on Earth . . . Wealth and riches will be in his house . . . He will guide his affairs with discretion . . . he will not be afraid of evil tidings"* (Psalm 112:1-3, 5, 7).

God's mercy: *"He has not dealt with us according to our sins, nor rewarded us according to our iniquities; for as the Heavens are high above the Earth, so great is His loving kindness toward those who fear Him"* (Psalm 103:10-11).

Guidance from the Holy Spirit: *"Who is the man who fears the Lord? He shall teach him in the way He chooses"* (Psalm 25:12).

Fulfilled desires and answered prayers: *"He will fulfill the desire of those who fear Him; He will also hear their cry and will save them"* (Psalm 145:19).

Protection by angels: *"The angel of the Lord encamps all around those who fear Him, and delivers them"* (Psalm 34:7-9).

Living a long life: *"The fear of the Lord prolongs days"* (Proverbs 10:27).

A place of safe refuge during adversity: *"In the fear of the Lord there is strong confidence, and his children will have a place of refuge"* (Proverbs 14:26).

Healing: *"But to you who fear My Name, the Son of Righteousness will rise with healing in His wings; and you will go out and grow fat like stall-fed calves"* (Malachi 4:2).

Firemen walk through the fires of adversity with courage because they understand the fear of the Lord. Firemen have learned to Man UP and control their environment through the fear of the Lord. That is when a man can become a true hero.

Controlling Our Environments

If we take a glass of water and cool it to thirty-two degrees Fahrenheit, we will get ice. If we take the same glass of water and heat it to two hundred twelve degrees Fahrenheit, we will get steam. We have the same substance—water—but its environment determines whether it will produce ice or steam. The same is true about you and me. We determine what our lifestyles will be like. Remember the old saying: "When life hands you a lemon, make lemonade!" There is truth to that adage.

Praise and worship will produce a life of joy and strength. Griping and groaning will produce a life of misery and weakness. We decide which environment in which to live. We can create a fireproof environment through praise and worship, or we can create an environment prone to calamity through negative speaking and thinking.

The presence of the Lord (the ultimate fireman) is within us. God's presence is released through praise and worship. God will not be found in griping and complaining. We come before God with singing, with praise, and with thankfulness. We are not griping about our circumstances; we are praising Him for His promises. We are creating our environment with praise! God inhabits the praise—not the gripes— of His people!

By praising God, we bring Him on the scene, and His presence brings the fullness of joy. That fullness of joy is our strength for overcoming the fires of adversity. When the joy of the Lord is gone, our strength is gone. We determine our strength by our praise, or we determine our weakness by griping. Praise and worship produces power for victory!

Trained to Believe

We have been trained to believe we must complain about the circumstances or nothing will ever be accomplished. This is a lie from the pit of hell! Do you know how elephants are trained? Have you ever seen huge elephants stand around docile and harmless, with only a small chain around their ankle that is attached to a puny stake stuck in the ground? Have you ever wondered why the huge elephant that weighs hundreds and hundreds of pounds doesn't just rip the chain and stake out of the ground and go off as he pleases?

It is because of the way the elephant was trained. When the elephant was a small baby, its trainer attached a huge, heavy chain around its foot. That chain was so rigged that when the elephant tried to escape and free itself from the chain, it would cut into its leg and inflict great pain. The harder he tried to get away, the more pain the chain inflicted. Finally, the elephant quit trying. He made up his mind that the chain and stake were his master, and they could not be beaten. Trying to escape causes pain, so the elephant never again tries to escape. After awhile, the trainer only has to use a small token chain and a portable stake, because in the elephant's mind, the chain is the master.

This perfectly illustrates why we must renew our minds to the truth that we create our own environment. We must learn that praise produces power for victory! Jesus taught that praise releases strength (see Psalm 8:1; Matthew 21:16). Praise releases the fireman in us.

A study of biblical languages shows us that the word that is used for *praise* in the Bible means, "to strengthen oneself inwardly." Praise strengthens us. Psalm 8 tells us God ordained praise because of our enemies. Through praise, God silences our enemies.

We become fireproof through praise and worship. When we Man UP and begin to praise and worship God, this positions us to become overcomers and heroes. Flex your strength as a man. Courageously praise and worship the Lord. The fireman within you will be released, and you will be a champion!

Chapter 8

The Rain Man

Tom Cruise and Dustin Hoffman performed par excellence in their roles in the movie *Rain Man*. It was one of my favorite movies, and we could certainly draw some life principles from the movie. But let's save that for another time.

In this chapter on the Rain Man, we could talk about the biblical concepts of the former rain and the latter rain being poured out on man in the last days (Hosea 6:3). As exciting as that would be, let's save that for another time as well.

In this chapter on the Rain Man, we certainly could do a play on words and discuss the fact that Jesus has made man to rule and *reign* as kings and priests in this life (Revelation 1:5-6, Romans 5:17). That would be a great study. This truth changed my life when I came to understand that Jesus has made me to be more than a conqueror. But we will save that discussion for another time as well.

I want to talk to you about rain and man. Why? Because it could not and did not rain on the earth until Adam knew how to Man UP. Originally, the earth did not experience rain. The earth was watered by a mist coming up from the ground

(Genesis 2:4-6). Why no rain? Scripture says in Genesis 2:6 that God did not cause it to rain because there was no man to cultivate the ground.

God did not send rain because man was not in position to cultivate the results of the rain. There was no one to Man UP enough to maintain the ground and reap the results of the rain, so God withheld the rain until He could get man in position. Someone had to Man UP before it could ever rain on the earth.

There had never been a downpour from heaven because there was no man in place to receive what God intended to give. Until we learn to Man UP, there are some things that God holds in the heavens waiting for us to be properly positioned as men. We may experience a little mist but not the downpour of favor and blessings God intends for us. This is why many men are frustrated and wonder why they are not further blessed in life than they are. When we have learned to Man UP in alignment with God, He will open the heavens and cause His favor and blessings to rain on us. It will be a downpour of heaven's favor and power released to us.

God is looking for a Rain Man. God is looking for men to be properly positioned to enjoy the downpour of His favor and blessings. You are to be the Rain Man. You can bring God's favor and blessings to you, your family, and your entire sphere of influence.

Becoming the Rain Man

My dad has been married four times to three different women. He married bride number two twice. I have been happily married to one wonderful woman for thirty-five years. Does that mean I am a better man than my dad is? NO! It simply means I learned how to be a rain man sooner than my dad learned. I have learned to position myself under the rain of God's outpouring on my life. I am most happy to tell you that my dad has also discovered how to stay positioned under the rain of God's favor pouring out on him. We laugh together as we look back and realize how one could learn to Man UP at any age, but for some it takes a few more bumps in the road. It is a joy to be able to report that today Dad is enjoying a happy, healthy marriage.

God waits for us to discover how to Man UP and become a rain man before He releases many of the blessings He intends for us to enjoy. Nobody can become a rain man for somebody else. We have to make the choice to become men. That choice is made when we decide to put away childish things. All of us want to be a rain man and live in the promises of God. To become a rain man, we must leave childhood and enter manhood. Paul talks about this in 1 Corinthians 13:11. He said, *"When I was a child, I spoke as a child, I understood as a child, I thought as a child; but when I became a man, I put away childish things."*

There are five specific reasons that we are unable to Man UP and position ourselves for God's favor. Becoming the rain man does not mean we are perfect men. The perfect man is like the guy who thought he was so great that he called dial-a-prayer and asked for his messages. There is no such thing as a perfect man. The perfect man only exists in a fool's mind! However, becoming a rain man is achievable. The rain man has made the choice to put away childish things and enter manhood.

Even Jesus had to leave childish things and grow into His

manhood before God released much of what was intended for Him (Luke 2:52). Jesus is our best example of a child becoming a man. He was a lion and a lamb. The rain man has learned to Man UP and possesses the natures of both the lion and the lamb. The rain man knows which nature to use and when to use it. As a lion, Jesus did some things He could not do as a lamb. If He had roared on the cross, He would have been weak. His strength at that moment was as a sacrificial Lamb. When Jesus comes again, it will be as a triumphant Lion with a roar (shout)! When we Man UP, we know which nature to call upon and how to use it.

While a young pastor, I had the privilege to travel with Dr. Ed Cole as his "young Timothy" in the early days of his ministry to men. When God gave Dr. Cole the revelation that older men are to mentor younger men, Dr. Cole took me as a young pastor into his trust. I often recall the day we were in Tulsa, Oklahoma, for one of Dr. Cole's men's rallies. While in the green room waiting to go to the platform, Dr. Cole introduced me to Pastor Billy Joe Daugherty. I don't know if Pastor Billy Joe recalls the meeting, but he referred to me as "the young Timothy" thereafter. That memory resonates in my heart. Dr. Cole taught us why men fall out of favor with God and cannot Man UP as the Rain Man. In his book, *Maximized Manhood*, he shared with us what five issues keep someone from the ability to Man UP and enjoy favor with God and man.

In 1 Corinthians 10:1-11, the Apostle Paul lists the five basic reasons why men cannot Man UP and enter their Promised Land. They are the reasons Israel failed to reach their Promised Land. They had to learn to leave these childish things and Man UP before they could enjoy the promises God had for them. Paul says these are written as our examples so we will experience God's favor, not His displeasure, and we will enter our Promised Land. In other words, Man UP, put these five childish things away, and you will become the rain man and enter your Promised Land.

Childhood or Manhood

The five childish things that kept Israel from God's favor and blessings and prevented them from entering the Promised Land are the same five reasons men miss out on true manhood today: lust, idolatry, sexual immorality, tempting Christ, and complaining. Let's get a quick understanding of what these childish sins are in today's world. (Sin means missing the mark, and these behaviors keep us from hitting the Man UP mark.)

1. **Lust** is not necessarily sexual. Lust is the preoccupation with what self wants. Lust is satisfying self at the expense of God and/or others. If I just care about satisfying myself and not my wife, that is lust. If a wife uses the credit card to run up bills her husband can't pay, that is lust. The difference between love and lust is that love gives and lust gets. Love satisfies another at my expense, while lust satisfies me at your expense.

We must choose to put away lust from our lives in order to Man UP and become the rain man. How? Keep reading, and we will give you instructions for putting away childish things at the close of this chapter. (Also review chapters five and six on how to be supercharged with God's power.)

2. **Idolatry** is when we esteem something more important than our devotion to God. Pornography is idolatrous. It is man creating a fantasy/image in his mind that satisfies him. Sports or our careers can become idols. Money or popularity can become idols. Idolatry keeps us from honoring God as our first love and denies us the ability to Man UP. We will not experience the rain of God's favor pouring down on our lives if we do not put away idolatry.

3. **Sexual immorality** is simply all types of sex sins. The Bible sets the standard for conduct that brings true fulfillment to all involved. God's promises are to him who overcomes (Revelation 3:5). When the men of Israel committed sexual immorality, they died in the wilderness and never entered their Promised Land. That was not God's plan then, and it is not God's plan now. We must put away sexual immorality and Man UP to enjoy all God has for us. This is possible. Keep reading and discover how.

4. **Tempting Christ** is demanding God to do something contrary to His Word or character. Some examples would be asking God to bless your finances, but you refuse to tithe. Tempting Christ would be to ask God to protect your family, but you refuse to provide for them. Tempting Christ would be asking God to bless your business while you lie and cheat to make deals. Tempting Christ is demanding that God provide some way of salvation other than the death, burial, and resurrection of Jesus Christ. We must put away wanting to enjoy the pleasures of sin and the benefits of salvation at the same time; this is tempting Christ.

5. **Complaining** is simply negative speaking. Criticizing,

faultfinding, and spreading rumors are all classified as complaining. Never finding the solution, we just complain about the problem and wonder why we never get ahead. We must get control of our tongues and put away complaining if we want to Man UP and experience God's best in our lives.

The Bible talks about the childish things that we must put away in order to Man UP.

> *Moreover, brethren, I do not want you to be unaware that all our fathers were under the cloud, all passed through the sea, all were baptized into Moses in the cloud and in the sea, all ate the same spiritual food, and all drank the same spiritual drink. For they drank of that spiritual Rock that followed them, and that Rock was Christ. But with most of them God was not well pleased, for their bodies were scattered in the wilderness. Now these things became our examples, to the intent that we should not lust after evil things as they also lusted. And do not become idolaters as were some of them. As it is written, "The people sat down to eat and drink, and rose up to play. Nor let us commit sexual immorality, as some of them did, and in one day twenty-three thousand fell; nor let us tempt Christ, as some of them also tempted, and were destroyed by serpents; nor complain, as some of them also complained, and were destroyed by the destroyer. Now all these things happened to them as examples, and they were written for our admonition* (1 Corinthians 10:1-11).

These verses were written for our admonition, which means urging, exhorting, or warning. We are warned that these five sins will keep us from the ability to Man UP and discover true purpose and fulfillment.

Getting What We Want

While discussing leaving childish things and how to Man UP with my good friend Pat Boone, he shared a couple of his experiences about positioning ourselves as rain men and enjoying God's favor.

Pat was on tour performing across the country. This was about the time of the Jim Bakker and Jimmy Swaggert moral controversies. One of the adult magazines had an article in it that Pat really wanted to read. His entire motivation, at first, was just to read this article. Pat did not want to hurt his testimony, but he wanted to read this article, so . . . he went to the gift shop of his hotel to purchase the magazine.

Pat looked all around to be sure no one recognized him as he slipped the magazine between some newspapers and walked to the cash register to pay for them. When he got to the cash register the cashier proclaimed, "You're Pat Boone, praise the Lord!" Pat said, "Excuse me, I forgot something" and he went back to the magazine rack and carefully, secretly, replaced the magazine hidden in his newspapers.

Pat returned to his room to change and go jogging, grateful that his almost purchase had not been detected. While Pat was jogging in a nearby park, he noticed a magazine had been tossed into the bushes. He went over to investigate. Not only was it the magazine with the article he wanted to read, but two other adult magazines in great condition were also lying in the bushes.

Pat picked up all three magazines and stuffed them into his jogging suit as he jogged back to the hotel. He wondered that maybe God had done this for him because he wanted to read the article but not hurt his testimony. When he arrived back at his room with the three magazines, he read the article. He decided at that time that he should not waste the other magazines, but he should look through them. It was at this moment that he paused and asked God if He had placed those magazines in the bushes for him to find. In this quiet moment, Pat heard the voice of the Lord say to him, *"That is what you wanted, wasn't it?"*

Conviction hit Pat like a ton of bricks. Pat instantly remembered that God gave Israel what they wanted, but it was not what God wanted. The result of God letting Israel have what they wanted was catastrophic (see 1 Samuel 8). Pat realized he was removing himself from God's favor by having those magazines. But that is not the end of the story.

Pat decided to destroy the magazines so they could not tempt any other men. He gathered the three magazines and went to the back of the hotel where they threw away all the hotel trash. He couldn't just toss them into the dumpster. He decided to burn them and toss them into the dumpster. As he was holding a burning magazine, about to toss it into the dumpster, out of nowhere came flashing lights and security police! Pat had to explain the whole story to them. Everything he tried to keep secret was now public. The security police let Pat go after he threw the magazines in the trash. Pat realized that as a man, he had to choose to put away childish things or they would become his master and destroy him.

On another day, Pat was at the airport waiting to board his plane. A large, muscular man grabbed Pat from behind and wrapped his arms around Pat. The man said, "I hear you want Ken Norton to break my jaw." Pat recognized the voice of Muhammad Ali, the world heavyweight boxing champion.

While being held in this loving, masculine hug, Pat replied, "Muhammad, you didn't hear the whole quote. I said I wanted Ken Norton to break your jaw so you would remember you are Clay. You were raised Cassius Clay. You changed your name to Muhammad to become a Muslim, and we Christians want you back."

Muhammad smiled at his friend and released him from his hug. They had a friendly conversation while waiting to board their flights. Muhammad asked Pat how he handled all the women that came with the fame.

Pat answered, "I use my faith. I remember that the Bible says that we are surrounded by a cloud of witnesses. Whatever we do, we are being observed by someone. Whatever we do, we are never alone. We are always on display. That helps me to properly handle the temptation and the fame." With that said, the time to board the planes came, and the two friends went their separate ways.

Muhammad Ali went on to win the fight with Ken Norton. However, during the fight, Ken Norton broke Muhammad Ali's jaw. Pat shared this story with me while reminding the two of us that we cannot let Satan get his hook in us. Jesus said, *"The ruler of this world has nothing in me"* (John 14:30). If we make the wrong choices and refuse to put away childish things, we let Satan get a fish hook in us. Satan will use it to pull on our flesh and reel us in to destruction. We must put away childish things and Man UP. Position yourself as a Rain Man and enjoy the downpour of God's favor and blessings in your life.

The Security System

People have security systems installed in their houses because of the valuables they contain, and sadly, we know that there are thieves who would like nothing better than to steal them. We learned that the five sins of lust, idolatry, sexual immorality, tempting Christ, and complaining will steal something valuable from us—our manhood. We need to install a security system that will alert us to their temptations and thereby keep them from stealing our manhood.

The security system that must be installed in our lives is praise and worship. Becoming involved in praise and worship is how we put away childish sins and Man UP. If we become caught up in a lifestyle of worship, those things that formerly kept us from true manhood will fade away!

In Mark 5, a man with an unclean spirit lived in the tombs and could not be tamed. He was so far gone that he would cry out and cut himself. The Bible says that when this man saw Jesus afar off, he ran and worshiped Jesus. He didn't get cleaned up before worshiping Jesus. He ran in his filthy condition to Jesus and began to worship Him.

While he worshiped Jesus, his filthy demons began to cry out to God. Demons have nothing to do with Jesus, but when a man worships Jesus, the demons will cry out. And Jesus will deliver us from our sins and cast the evil spirits out of our lives! Praise and worship bring the presence of Jesus, and the evil spirits are tormented. As we worship Jesus, the security alarm goes off, and His presence will drive out the evil spirits.

The greatest releases I have experienced have been on my knees and with my hands lifted to God in praise and worship

(Psalm 63:4). I remember when my children were babies learning to walk. For some reason, when learning to walk, they would raise their hands straight up to give them a sense of balance. When we raise our hands to God in praise and worship, we find a new balance for life and are better able to walk in the Spirit. No matter how tired I was when I saw my children coming towards me with their hands raised in the air, I couldn't help but pick them up, love them, and encourage them to keep walking. Jesus does the same for us! As we praise and worship Jesus for His example of manhood and His great love, we are filled with His presence and enabled to put away childish things.

The Power of Praise and Worship

I accepted an invitation to hear Troy Perry, the founder of the Metropolitan Church, speak at a church my son was attending. I love my son and wanted to know what he was involved with, so I agreed to attend the evening service.

During his message, Troy Perry made much eye contact with me. I sensed he knew me and wanted to get acquainted. After the close of the message, he made a valiant effort to get to me (before I could leave my pew and get into the aisle). He shook my hand and put his arm around my shoulder; as we entered the aisle, he invited my wife and me to go back to the fellowship hall and enjoy some refreshments with him and the other ministers. I was uncomfortable. I looked up as we walked down the aisle, and there was a major network news camera filming this event. It was national gay pride day, and I did not know it! God has some sense of humor.

Anyway, the reason I am sharing this event is because I

analyzed everything that took place at this service. I was nervous and embarrassed (by my traditions), but I wanted to know if my son was safe while he worshiped at this church. To my amazement, during the time of corporate praise and worship, the most awesome awareness of the presence of God was very tangible. I inquired of the Lord as to why and what was happening. I heard the Lord say, *"I inhabit the praises of my people. Praise and worship releases a purity of love and power. These men and women are crying out to me in their pain through their praise and worship, and I love them and fill them with My love as they worship Me. That is what you are experiencing."*

Praise and worship is a power release. As we praise and worship God, we are positioned for Him to rain down His love and empower us to put away childish things. I do not believe this is a one-time fix but an ongoing lifestyle require-ment for true manhood. As we discussed before, overcoming involves due process. Praise and worship is a key to this process. As I praise and worship God, I am enabled to Man UP and be an overcomer!

Why not Man UP right now? Make the choice to put away childish things. Without embarrassment, lift up your hands to God and tell Him you desire to put away childish things. You want to Man UP. Thank Him for His mercy and loving-kindness. Honor Him for all He is. He will rain down His love and power on you. You are an overcomer through Jesus Christ. You are the rain man, and you are entering the promised land God has for you!

Chapter 9

The Repair Man

I purchased a beautiful, previously owned, black Infiniti Q45. It was a joy to drive. It had all the bells and whistles; however, the transmission began to shift irregularly. I took the car to the repairman recommended by my mechanic. The repairman was a proven, trustworthy man with reasonable prices for his repair work. He informed me that I needed a new transmission. Ugh! I agreed to have a used transmission put in because it was less expensive, and the Q45 drove with precision once again.

My wife, Darlene, had become good friends with Tammy Faye Messner (formerly Tammy Faye Bakker) and her husband Roe. At this time in his life, Roe was serving a two-year prison sentence. Darlene and I were most happy to be able to drive Tammy on the several hour road trips to the prison to visit with her husband. We felt God was pleased with our willingness to serve. So, I was shocked when on a return trip home from Roe and Tammy's house, the new transmission in my Q45 went kerplunk. It overheated and everything inside melted. In the wee hours of the morning,

Darlene and I sat stranded in our beautiful Q45 on the side of the freeway in a scary neighborhood. I had a few thoughts about the repairman and the transmission he had installed . . . and a few questions for God.

A second transmission had to be installed (and purchased). In hindsight, I understand that it was not the repairman's fault. It was the used equipment I agreed to have installed. The repairman warned me against a used transmission, but I chose the less expensive used transmission. We should listen to proven repairmen, especially when they are proven as people of integrity.

On another occasion, I was in Phoenix, Arizona, on a business trip. It was one hundred and five plus degrees. I knew that if I moved a little slower and drank plenty of water, I would get through this trip okay despite the hot weather. I was going through a very stressful time in my career, and this trip was important for future income. However, pain occasionally shot through my chest. I attributed the pains to the stress I was dealing with and pressed forward.

After returning home from the trip, the pain in my chest continued. My wife insisted that I go to a cardiologist for a checkup. I refused. I didn't want to spend the time or the money. However, she would not let me reason away my pain. I went for a stress test, and the results were inconclusive, so I figured it was nothing. Because the chest pains continued and increased in frequency, Darlene scheduled an appointment for me to have a nuclear test done that would be very specific. The results indicated a blockage to my heart. It was a Friday afternoon, and my cardiologist was unable to do angioplasty, which was necessary to confirm the suspicions, so he arranged for me to go to Scripps in La Jolla, California, to an internationally recognized surgeon in cardiology. The appointment was for the following Monday. I was told by my cardiologist not do to do anything strenuous and to keep a phone nearby with access to 911. These instructions did not help my stress level.

That Monday while I was on the surgery table and the angioplasty diagnosis was in process, the doctor informed me that I had three options. Option number one was I could go home and do nothing, and within 30 days, I would be dead. The left side of my heart was completely shut down. Only God was keeping me alive.

Option number two was open heart surgery. I would be in the hospital for six weeks, but the results would probably be very good.

He informed me that option number three was "no slam dunk." In fact, the doctor told me that only ten percent of hospitals in the world would even attempt this option, and of that ten percent, only two percent would be successful. However, the doctor was confident they could help me if I would choose this option.

I had to decide to trust the repairman (doctor) God had supernaturally brought into my life (through a series of circumstances) for a risky procedure into what they call "dead man's triangle" of my heart or face death. It was time to Man UP.

With all the courage and faith I could muster, I selected option number three and went for the risky procedure. If it failed, they would rush me into open heart surgery (the room and staff were standing ready) and do some bypass work. Praise the Lord, within a short time, the procedure was successful, and today I am healthy!

100 Percent Guaranteed

As men, the possibility of our needing repair is one hundred percent! God understands our weaknesses; after all, He created us. He said He remembers our frame, and He knows that we are just dust (Psalm 103:14).

The need for repair can be minor, or it can devastate us. Failure to turn on the heat in a house can make us uncomfortable. However, failure to put down the landing gear of an airplane can kill us! We have all experienced different levels of need for repairs.

Jesus also endured repairs. Scripture says He grew in wisdom and stature and favor with God and man (Luke 2:52). Moreover, Jesus was constantly the repairman. In some relationships He repaired the problems or damages such as His relationship with Peter after Peter denied him (John 21:15-21). Yet in another situation, God divorced Israel as the method of repair (Jeremiah 3:6-8). It is noteworthy that without God's repair action of divorcing Israel and remarrying another bride, there would be no such thing as the church or Christianity today. Sometimes divorce may be God's repair answer. God in His great love has not forgotten Israel. He has a plan for Israel's restoration. My point is that methods of repair are varied. Some relationships can be repaired while others may need to be replaced.

Jesus said He was the gardener, and we are His field. He is constantly pruning us to enable us to bear more fruit. If we do not bear fruit, there comes a time when we are lopped off from the vine (John 15:1-8). Jesus, as the repairman, uses restoration when possible, and He uses removal or replacement as methods of repair when necessary. We will have to

Man UP and listen to the Holy Spirit to discern the correct procedure for the repairs necessary.

Repairmen are necessary for life. Obviously, there are many types of repair that may be required. However, did you know that God has called and equipped you to be a repairman (Isaiah 58:12)? God delights in our being recognized as repairmen of integrity who properly restore, rebuild, remove, and/or replace damaged or faulty relationships and issues in our lives (Isaiah 58:12). Some relationships can be repaired; others must be replaced.

As repairmen of integrity, we must understand both the severity and the goodness of God (Romans 11:19-23; Acts 9:31). Through intimacy with the Holy Spirit, we will be given strategies. Some of the strategies will seem severe, and some will seem kind. As we Man UP and prepare for our role as repairmen, it will be through obedience to the strategies that the necessary repairs will take place. As repairmen, we and those we help will discover purpose and fulfillment in life.

Guaranteed Success as Repairmen

As repairmen we must understand that reproof is the way of life (Proverbs 6:23; Proverbs 13:18). A reproof needs to be done with love, courageously pointing out the problem and the reason that problem exists, **with possible solutions**. The solutions will be the Holy Spirit strategies/principles that, when obeyed, produce the desired results. If possible solutions are not offered, it is not a reproof but a criticism without any power to change anything.

You may wonder, "How could I be used by God as a

repairman? I have enough personal problems that need to be repaired." One of my favorite passages of Scripture is a promise that guarantees us success as repairmen, for both our personal problems and for helping others. It is found in Proverbs 2:

> For the LORD grants wisdom! From his mouth come knowledge and understanding. He grants a treasure of good sense to the godly. He is their shield, protecting those who walk with integrity. He guards the paths of justice and protects those who are faithful to him. Then you will understand what is right, just, and fair and **you will know how to find the right course of action every time.** For wisdom will enter your heart, and knowledge will fill you with joy (Proverbs 2:6-10 NLT, emphasis added).

We are promised that God will give us the ability to choose the right course of action every time—not some of the time, but hallelujah, *every time!*

The Repairman's Tool Box

Jesus used reproof as His tool for repairs (Revelation 2:2-6; 13-14; 19-20). A reproof is a correction, which includes the strategy for the necessary repair. A reproof explains the error and its ultimate outcome, and offers a correct action that will bring about righteous results. After Jesus gave a reproof, He waited for the response. Repentance is always the right response. Repentance is simply agreeing with God and making the necessary changes the repair demands.

The response to the reproof (repair strategy) determines if the repair will be successful. The response determines if a relationship can be repaired and restored, or if it must be replaced. For example, Jesus taught that if there is no repentance, then there can be no forgiveness (Luke 17:3). Jesus said to give others a second opportunity, but if there is not the proper response to the reproof (repair strategy), have nothing more to do with the person or situation (Titus 3:10).

As repairmen, we must understand two aspects of Jesus: the *person* of Jesus Christ, whom we first came to know at salvation, and the *principles* of Jesus Christ, which are contained in the Bible.

When we are born again, we enter into a relationship with the person of Jesus Christ. He is the Son of God, born of a virgin, who lived a sinless life and went about doing good (Acts 10:38). Jesus died on the cross for our sins. He was buried in a tomb, but three days later God raised Him from the dead. He ascended into heaven and is now seated at the right hand of the Father, working on our behalf (Romans 10:9).

Many have responded to the call and have received the free gift of eternal life through Jesus, and now know the person, Jesus Christ. However, many believers have not gone on to pursue the principles that Jesus taught us to live by, which are contained in God's Word, the Bible.

My circumstances don't change overnight right after I was born again. For example, if I was overweight when I accepted Jesus Christ as my Savior, I was still overweight immediately after I accepted Him. My salvation was secured. I was on my way to heaven, but nothing changed in my physical circumstances. The circumstances only change as I discover and obey the principles found in the Scriptures. As I choose to obey the Scriptures, the person Jesus Christ, through the Holy Spirit, gives me the ability/anointing to achieve righteous results. The ability or the anointing is released through my actions. If I do not attempt to accomplish the principle (follow the repair strategy), there will be no anointing for the desired results.

Jesus is more than just a personal Savior; He is the Word made flesh. We can never know Him fully, nor experience the blessings derived from intimacy with Him unless we first receive and apply the principles of the Word of God in our lives! Those principles, when acted upon, become the keys of the kingdom that unlock the resources of heaven to bring victory and blessings to our lives. His principles are the repairman's tool box.

For example, let's say a mailman was enjoying his work until one day he was bitten by a dog while delivering the mail. This caused the mailman much alarm. A supervisor (repairman) instructed the mailman that one of his available tools was a can of Mace. The supervisor said that if any dog tried to bite him, he should spray the dog with the Mace, and the dog would be sorry for trying to hurt the mailman. The next time a dog tried to bite the mailman, he used his can of Mace. To his delight, the dog went yelping away in a hurry. This newly found authority so delighted the mailman that he went around the whole neighborhood looking for dogs that might be a nuisance. At any opportunity he could find, the mailman would blast the dogs with his Mace. He was thrilled at his newfound power. However, there was a problem. The mailman became so preoccupied with his newly discovered authority of getting rid of the dogs with Mace that he forgot to deliver the mail!

Men, we can easily get sidetracked with the exciting adventure of manhood, but we must not forget that we will be called upon to perform as repairmen. We can accomplish the repairs necessary through the principles of the Word of God. Our purpose as men is not to go around looking for ways to show off our power (spraying the Mace). Our purpose is to cultivate intimacy with the Holy Spirit. The Holy Spirit will equip us to rule and reign—to Man UP. He will train us in the proper use of the Mace.

Problems Reveal the Quality of Our Manhood

Through the process of serving as a repairman, you will discover the joy that comes when you Man UP. Problems reveal the quality of our manhood. Problems are the catalysts for discovering purpose and fulfillment in life. The Bible is full of examples of people who recognized their purpose by solving problems (being repairmen). Moses solved problems for the Israelites. Aaron solved problems for Moses. Jonathon solved problems for David. Mechanics solve car problems. Dentists solve tooth problems. Accountants solve tax problems. God created us to solve problems. Solving problems is what releases our manhood.

Each one of us is a solution. We are repairmen by nature. You are a problem solver—a repairman—for someone. You may be the healer for somebody who is sick. You may be a life jacket for someone drowning. You may be a ruler for someone out of control. You may be the lifter for someone depressed. You are a reward to someone! Somebody needs you. Somebody wants you. You are necessary to somebody, somewhere, as their repairman (Jeremiah 1:4-5).

You were created for a specific purpose, to repair a specific problem on earth. This is a key to understanding how to Man UP. God is not a respecter of persons. He created Jeremiah for a special time and season, and for a special people. It is the same with each of us.

Somebody needs you. Moses was needed as a leader to the children of Israel. David was needed by the Israelites to defeat Goliath. David was a repairman for King Saul as well. Pharaoh desperately needed someone to interpret his dream. Joseph was a repairman to him. Every man God created is a repairman for somebody.

It is also important to recognize that there are other people who do not really need you. You are not their answer. You are not their solution. Do not be offended by this. God has somebody else planned for them. You are not needed everywhere. You are only needed at a specific place, at a specific time, and for a specific person or people.

The people who need your repair skills may not initially see you as being their repairman, but you really are. You are exactly what God has ordered for their lives. It is the responsibility of others to discern you as the repairman God has given to them. The Pharisees did not discern that Jesus was their repairman, but Zacchaeus did, and a life-changing relationship was born. Even Pharaoh of Egypt, an unbeliever, discerned that Joseph was the answer to the dilemma of his dream.

If you are not recognized as a repairman, do not be dismayed. God will bring you to the right situation at the right time (Ecclesiastes 3:1-8). As repairmen, we may fall or cut our knuckles, but we will not fail because God has us by the hand (Psalm 37:23-24). We do not have Him by the hand, but it is He who holds onto our hands and never loses His grip. That is why we are guaranteed victory as repairmen (2 Corinthians 2:14).

Invisible Instructions for the Repairman

As a repairman, you come with instructions. I learned this principle from Mike Murdock. Instructions may be unknown, ignored, or distorted, but they do exist. These instructions are invisible yet cannot be doubted. Examine an apple seed carefully. Look inside the apple seed. Analyze it. If you try for a lifetime to locate the instruction to produce apples, you will not find it. Those instructions are not visible. Yet, the command cannot be doubted. Plant a million apple seeds, and none of them will ever produce a watermelon.

The instructions for us as a repairman are already defined. They cannot be refuted. The product is the proof. Within everything created is a desire and command to produce, increase, and multiply. Something within us wants to repair a problem for someone, somewhere, sometime. Exercising this desire for repairs releases our manhood and brings fulfillment.

Through intimacy with the Holy Spirit, our repairman ability becomes known to ourselves and to others. The Holy Spirit is totally focused on us (Psalm 139:3). We are never outside His reach (Psalm 139:1-18). It is impossible to count the pleasurable thoughts that pour from the Holy Spirit toward us every day. Even in our darkest moments, the Holy Spirit will turn on the light for us to enable us to be successful repairmen.

Valued Repairman

During the sixties, the economy was booming, yet Dunn and Bradstreet reported an average of more than thirteen thousand business failures annually. Researchers discovered that the reason for the majority of these failures (almost 92 percent) were due to management difficulties. Facts don't lie; business institutions don't fail until the leaders do.

Have you ever gone into a restaurant that at one time had a great reputation, but now you were disappointed? Instead of being elegant, it looked run down and unkempt. You anticipated great service and atmosphere but the experience disappointed you. You realized that the problem wasn't a bad cook or bad server or hostess; it was the management who was responsible. Sometimes you can sense it when you walk into a place and say to yourself, *This place needs a repairman. It needs a makeover.*

If you are a football fan like me, you've noticed teams can go from first place to the cellar in one season. Many times, it was because they needed a new coach/repairman. When the repairman came in and turned things around, the team once again started to win championships.

Perhaps you are old enough to remember when Chrysler decided to do something about its decline in the American market. They did not change the body style of the cars or ask the dealers to change the look of their dealerships. They hired a repairman—Lee Iacocca. In just a short time, he became as famous as his former boss, Henry Ford. The repairman, Iacocca, turned the company around.

While I was a squad leader in the Air Force, I experienced a flight team that completely reversed itself from having very low morale and performance to one with great camaraderie and high productivity. The team made the transformation because a new Flight Commander (repairman) took charge. As a pastor, I have seen entire churches change from being a congregation in decline to one that is growing and making a difference in the community when the pastor (repairman) took the reins of responsibility.

The value of a repairman cannot be denied, especially in your home. The atmosphere in the entire house can change the moment you, the repairman, return home. You, the loving, confident repairman, can make the difference. The right repairman is highly valued!

Man UP and understand your role as a repairman. Look for opportunities to heal, strengthen, and bless others. Do good every time it is possible (Proverbs 3:37). God has specifically prepared events and situations for you as a repairman (1 Corinthians 2:9). You will be equipped to choose the right course of repair every time (Proverbs 2:6-9).

You will discern where you are needed as a repairman by the Holy Spirit (1 Corinthians 2:10). Accomplishing your role as a repairman requires your obedience and cooperation (Deuteronomy 28:1). The Holy Spirit decides what and when He desires you to be the repairman. You decide your obedience or disobedience to Him. That is why our relationship with the Holy Spirit is an absolute necessity.

God knows you have the ability to bring in an award-winning performance as a repairman. He is brilliant. If you were not capable of accomplishing the repairs, He would not have placed the desire, ability, and instructions within you. You may feel incapable—Moses did (Exodus 3:11). You may feel weak and inarticulate—Paul did (1 Corinthians 2:3-4). You may feel unworthy—Paul did (Ephesians 3:7-8). You may feel foolish—Paul did (1 Corinthians 1:27). You may feel powerless and without clout—David did (Psalm 5:12). It doesn't matter how you feel; it is because of the Holy Spirit in you that you are qualified as a repairman.

The Repair Man

You are called as a repairman to restore someone or something that is damaged or faulty to a good condition. As an anointed repairman, you will be greatly rewarded. When you Man UP and operate as an anointed repairman, God promises that it will be more than worth it. He promises you a double reward for your trouble (Isaiah 61:7).

Every day is an exciting adventure. You may be called upon today as an anointed repairman. The Holy Spirit in you is ready! God is not looking at your outward appearances—He is looking at your heart. Keep it pure before Him. Pursue Him daily and with great diligence. Remember, you can do all things through Christ! (Philippians 4:13). In His presence, you become qualified as a skilled repairman.

The Holy Spirit in you will give you the strategies needed for the repairs to whatever is damaged or broken in your life or the lives of those you love. As you follow the repair strategies, you will experience the Holy Spirit come upon you and empower you for a successful repair. Man UP and press on to the next role you will be called upon to perform!

119

Chapter 10

The Combat Man

I always wanted to fly. I knew that the ladies like men in uniform, so when I was young I dreamed about joining the Air Force and becoming a pilot. I took two years of ROTC (Reserved Officers Training Corp). Fresh out of high school, I enlisted in the United States Air Force. I knew I was about to be drafted and not have a choice in the branch of service I desired. I wanted to learn to fly and knew I had a better chance of doing so if I joined the Air Force. I enlisted and did receive my pilot's training. I was trained during my own off-duty time by an Air Force pilot. I did not become an Air Force fighter pilot, but I got as close as I could to doing so, and my wife tells me I did look good in uniform.

Should I have been obligated to serve if I had been drafted into another branch of service? Is military duty a responsibility of man? What about the draft system and required combat duty? These are valid questions today because America is at war! We are at war with terrorism. America will never be the same since 9/11. America has had to Man UP and defend herself.

How should we as men respond to times of war and military conflict? What is God's standard and requirement for man during military conflicts? Must I Man UP and go to combat, or can I Man UP and not have to experience it?

Let's discover some power principles about the combat man and the role you may be called upon to perform. These principles will make you more than a conqueror and give you the ability to perform as a combat man without fear. Let's begin by looking at the war on terrorism. Then we will talk about each man's personal wars.

Principle: There is a time for war! God declares there is a season for every purpose He has planned.

There is a time for everything, a season for every activity under heaven. A time to be born and a time to die. A time to plant and a time to harvest. A time to kill and a time to heal . . . A time to love and a time to hate. A time for war and a time for peace (Ecclesiastes 3:1-8).

God Himself had to go to war. He was not able to negotiate peace in heaven. Combat was inevitable even in heaven (Revelation 12:7).

Men, we must understand our righteous response when it is God's time for war! He had to go to war with Satan and 1/3 of heaven was affected by this war! (Actually all of heaven went to war and 1/3 of heaven was punished by it.)

Then I saw heaven opened, and a white horse was standing there. And the one sitting on the horse was named Faithful and True. For he judges fairly and then goes to war (Revelation 19:11).

Principle: War is not always a judgment of God. The war in heaven was not God's judgment on heaven. The war in heaven was the result of evil. War was the remedy to the evil that had been released. Peace could not be negotiated in heaven. America's war on terrorism is the result of evil men under the influence of Satan. Peace cannot be negotiated with terrorists. Terrorists must be removed from the planet just as they were from heaven.

Ecclesiastes 8:14 tells us that sometimes something useless happens on earth. Bad things happen to good people, and good things happen to bad people. It is important to understand that what happened on September 11, 2001 was not God's will. This world is not under His control. First John 5:19 says, *"We know that we are children of God and that the world around us is under the power and control of the evil one."* God has given man the mandate to Man UP and take dominion and fill the earth with righteousness because there has always been an enemy that must be overcome (Genesis 1:26-28).

Righteousness will prevail. Remember the cities of Sodom and Gomorrah? These were relatively sick places. So sick, in fact, that God ultimately decided to destroy them as an act of judgment. Abraham stepped in and asked, "Wait a minute, if I can find ten righteous people, would you save the city?" God said, "Absolutely!" These cities could be spared by the righteousness of the ten. Unfortunately he could not find even ten righteous men. (Certainly, there must be at least ten righteous men in America.)

Righteousness will prevail. God in His love sent man a Savior. When we accept the Savior and learn to live by His kingdom principles, righteousness will prevail. Terrorists will be overcome.

An obvious question is this: Could God have stopped the terrorists? Sure, He could have; it would have been easy. All He would have to do is take away their free will, removing their power to choose. He could do that. However, for Him to be just (which God always is), He'd have to take away your free will and my free will too. He doesn't want to do that because He loves us too much. The greatest power God gave to us is the power to choose. It is also our greatest weakness because we often choose unwisely. And whenever people choose unwisely, innocent people suffer. When a parent chooses to be abusive, an innocent child suffers. When doctors choose to suck the life out of a million pre-born children every year, the most innocent among us suffer.

God never forces His will on anyone. Jesus told us in John 8:44 that the devil and his followers are murderers and liars. It ought to be obvious whom the individuals who attacked America are really serving. It makes it clear that this attack was not God's will nor God's judgment. It was the will of evil individuals.

Did the people killed in the World Trade Center collapse and the airplanes crashing happen to these people because they were in sin? Jesus was asked this question about disaster killing people in His day. Read Jesus' answer:

About this time Jesus was informed that Pilate had murdered some people from Galilee as they were sacrificing at the Temple in Jerusalem. "Do you think those Galileans were worse sinners than other people from Galilee?" he asked. "Is that why they suffered? Not at all! And you will also perish unless you turn from your evil ways and turn to God. And what about the eighteen men who died when the Tower of Siloam fell on them? [Sounds like the WTC and Pentagon] *Were they the worst sinners in Jerusalem? No, and I tell you again that unless you repent, you will also perish"* (Luke 13:1-5).

Disasters, such as the WTC and Pentagon crashes, are not God's punishment! They are the result of evil men under Satan's influence. Jesus said all men will die without everlasting life if they do not have Jesus as Savior.

The Laws of War

God does not choose sides among men. Man must be on the side of God. His purpose is what counts (see Joshua 5:1-13).

The Lord is my light and my salvation—so why should I be afraid? The Lord protects me from danger—so why should I tremble? When evil people come to destroy me, when my enemies and foes attack me, they will stumble and fall. Though a mighty army surrounds me, my heart will know no fear. Even if they attack me, I remain confident (Psalm 27:1-3).

God does give man skill for warfare.

Bless the LORD, who is my rock. He gives me strength for war and skill for battle. He is my loving ally and my fortress, my tower of safety, my deliverer. He stands before me as a shield, and I take refuge in him. He subdues the nations under me (Psalm 144:1-2).

In order to Man UP we must be trained and understand God's principles of warfare!

The Lord left certain nations in the land to train those Israelites who had not participated in the wars of Canaan. He did this to teach warfare to generations of Israelites who had no experience in battle (Judges 3:1-4).

We can Man UP and go to war without fear through obedience to God! Skill in war and victory in war come from God.

There were 44,760 skilled warriors in the armies of Reuben, Gad, and the half-tribe of Manasseh. They were all skilled in combat and armed with shields, swords, and bows. They waged war against the Hagrites . . . They cried out to God during the battle, and he answered their prayer because they trusted in him. So the Hagrites and all their allies were defeated . . . Many of the Hagrites were killed in the battle because God was fighting against them (1 Chronicles 5:18-22).

Three Strikes, You're Out!

When God goes to war, He follows three steps before He attacks. To properly Man UP for our performance as a combat man, we need to understand and adhere to these three steps.

1. God sends His priests (pastors) to minister courage to the people through prayer. God offers a chance for peace to the enemy. Grace always precedes judgment, but too often we mistake the grace as weakness.

2. God lays out the terms for the enemy to avoid war with Him.

3. He gives them a display of His strength. If they refuse His terms, He must blow them ALL off the map, sparing nothing and no one! These three steps are clearly explained in the book of Deuteronomy.

> *When you go out to fight your enemies and you face horses and chariots and an army greater than your own, do not be afraid. The LORD your God, who brought you safely out of Egypt, is with you! Before you go into battle, the priest will come forward to speak with the troops. He will say, "Listen to me, all you men of Israel! Do not be afraid as you go out to fight today! Do not lose heart or panic . . ." As you approach a town to attack it, first offer its people terms for peace. If they accept your terms and open the gates to you, then all the people inside will serve you in forced labor. But if they refuse to make peace and prepare to fight, you must attack the town. When the LORD your God hands it over to you, kill every man in the town . . . "As for the towns of the nations the LORD your God is giving you as a special possession, destroy every living thing in them. You must completely destroy the Hittites, Amorites, Canaanites, Perizzites, Hivites, and Jebusites, just as the LORD your God has commanded you. This will keep the people of the land from teaching you their detestable customs in the worship of their gods, which would cause you to sin deeply against the LORD your God"* (Deuteronomy 20:1-18).

Principle: Calling up the reserves and instituting a draft system is God's wisdom for war time.

Take a census of the whole community of Israel by their clans and families. List the names of all the men twenty

126

years old or older who are able to go to war. You and Aaron are to direct the project (Numbers 2:1-3).

The combat man must be prepared for battle. There is only one exception to the draft during war. *"A newly married man must not be drafted into the army or given any other special responsibilities. He must be free to be at home for one year, bringing happiness to the wife he has married"* (Deuteronomy 24:5). Bringing happiness to your wife is another book in itself. I'm sure you will be happy bringing happiness to your new bride. Then it is off to war.

The combat man understands that conscientious objectors are not biblical. Objectors birth discouragement among the troops and should be avoided.

> *"Do you mean you want to stay back here while your brothers go across and do all the fighting?" Moses asked the Reubenites and Gadites. "Are you trying to discourage the rest of the people of Israel from going across to the land the LORD has given them?"* (see Numbers 32:1-23).

How Man Should Respond to Terrorists

The Bible tells us how to respond to terrorist attacks. In 1 Samuel 30, David and his men arrived home and found that terrorists had raided and burned Ziklag to the ground. Terrorists had taken the women and children as slaves. David cried out to God for how he should respond. (You really should read the entire story because you will be encouraged.) I have discovered four responses from this story.

1. The first response is found in 1 Samuel 30:4. *"So David*

and his men wept aloud until they had no strength left to weep"
(NIV). We too should **grieve over loss**. We should feel the
pain and understand the five phases of the grieving process—
shock, realization, retreat, transition, and then recovery.

Shock says we can't believe this is happening. Then we
move to *realization* where we begin to accept the facts. This
leaves us restless and brings conflicting emotions of hopeless-
ness and anger, which give way to frustration, followed by
denial, then fear, and finally hate. Sometimes all those
emotions are felt at the same time. From these, we move into
retreat. Retreat is the stage where you say to yourself, "I just
need to be alone. I need to think how my life will change."
This leads us to the next phase, *transition*. Transition is when
our hope returns to us. We begin to believe that life might be
worth living again. We start to see some of the good things
that could still happen. These emotions build one upon
another until we move into the final phase, *recovery*. Recovery
is when we can remember the good times without breaking
down. We can remember the joy before the tragedy. Recovery
is when we understand that although things will never be the
same, we are still willing to move forward. The entire process
of grieving can take days, weeks, or months.

2. The second response, **bitterness and rage**, is found in 1
Samuel 30:6. *"David was greatly distressed because the men were
talking of stoning him; each one was bitter in spirit because of his
sons and daughters. But David found strength in the LORD his
God"* (NIV). David had done nothing wrong, but the people
wanted to kill him because he was their leader. Why? When
people feel powerless and suffer serious loss, they become so
uncomfortable they must blame someone. Bitterness and

misplaced rage are always destructive and cause people to make poor decisions. It is bitterness that makes it possible for people to do the unthinkable. So no matter what happens, don't allow yourself to grow bitter. *"See to it that no one misses the grace of God and that no bitter root grows up to cause trouble and defile many"* (Hebrews 12:15).

When times are tough, our greatest source of strength is in the Lord. First Samuel 30 tells us that when the terrorists attacked, David found his strength in the Lord. Aren't we glad that God doesn't play hard to get at times like this? Aren't we glad He isn't in heaven saying, "Oh, now you want to come talk to me?" God is gracious. Psalm 96:2 tells us God is our protection and our strength. He always helps in times of trouble, so we should not be afraid even if the earth shakes or the mountains fall into the sea.

3. The third response for a combat man is found in 1 Samuel 30:8. "And David inquired of the LORD, "Shall I pursue this raiding party? Will I overtake them?" "Pursue them," he answered. "You will certainly overtake them and succeed in the rescue." We must **seek divine direction**. We must pray! Pray for a spirit of repentance and revival in America. Pray for our leadership, for example, to have supernatural insight on how to deal with terrorists.

4. The fourth response I find in this story is **the government takes decisive action**. The purpose of government is to protect the citizens. In the 1 Samuel 30 account we have been looking at, David was the governing leader of the people when terrorists attacked their homeland. After David prayed, he received God's direction, and he acted. He made a plan and put it into motion. David responded quickly! And finally,

in verse 17 we see that David administered justice to the terrorists. *"David fought them from dusk until the evening of the next day, and none of them got away, except four hundred young men who rode off on camels and fled."* He slaughtered them.

A combat man understands that his government will have a strategy for victory.

Romans 13:1-4 says,

> *Obey the government, for God is the one who put it there. All governments have been placed in power by God. So those who refuse to obey the laws of the land are refusing to obey God, and punishment will follow. For the authorities do not frighten people who are doing right, but they frighten those who do wrong. So do what they say, and you will get along well. The authorities are sent by God to help you. But if you are doing something wrong, of course you should be afraid, for you will be punished. The authorities are established by God for that very purpose, to punish those who do wrong.*

The primary purpose of government is to establish peace, provide justice, and protect the people. The government is to be a minister of God to bring justice and carry out punishment upon those who practice evil. God has designed the government as the arm of His authority for justice. There is nothing immoral about a government striking down evil. In fact it is required, and those who engage in evil should be fearful because the government does not use the sword (or the cruise missile) for nothing.

To summarize, the combat man's four responses to terrorists should be:

1) Grieve.

2) Beware of misplaced bitterness and rage.

3) Find strength in God. Pray for divine wisdom.

4) Let God use the government to respond quickly with a plan and administer justice.

As combat men, we are resolved to the removal of terrorists. We pray for a spirit of confusion to fall upon all those who would embrace this kind of godless, murderous activities. May their wisdom fail them. May they make mistakes and be brought to justice. And let us pray for all those who lost loved ones due to terrorist acts. May God flood them with peace and comfort.

Psalm 91 says not to fear because God is our habitation. Let us be courageous and comforted because we are on the Lord's side!

The Lord Almighty is here among us; the God of Israel is our fortress. Come, see the glorious works of the Lord. See how he brings destruction upon the world and causes wars to end throughout the earth. He breaks the bow and snaps the spear in two; he burns the shields with fire. "Be silent, and know that I am God! I will be honored by every nation. I will be honored throughout the world." The Lord Almighty is here among us; the God of Israel is our fortress (Psalm 46:7-11).

As combat men, we can be confident that God will show us how to do battle and be victorious. And we must be men of prayer. We must pray for our leaders and those in the military. We must pray for all those affected by war. As we pray, let us remember that our God reigns, and righteousness will prevail!

The Man UP Uniform

The story is told of a little boy who came home from school all dirty with his clothes torn. He remarked to his mom as he walked into the house, "That was a good fight."

The mother saw her son's black eye, torn jeans, and scrapes and asked, "What was so good about it?"

He replied, "I won!"

The Bible tells us to fight the good fight of faith (1 Timothy 6:12). A good fight is the fight we win! As men, we must recognize that we will always have an enemy. This mandates that we know how to perform as combat men because sometime we will have to Man UP and fight a good fight. Remember, even God could not negotiate peace. He had a fight in heaven, and there were casualties. One third of the angels of heaven were cast out with Satan (Revelation 12:7-9).

As men, we will never outgrow warfare so we must learn to fight. We will fall from time to time, but great men always get back up (Psalm 37:23-24). Satan only attacks those he fears most. You know how to Man UP. You are more than a conqueror and do not have to fear his attacks. Through fellowship with the Holy Spirit, you are equipped to annihilate all enemies (2 Corinthians 2:14).

The Bible tells us in Ephesians 6 to put on our entire uniform, the armor of God. We are to put on the uniform because it enables us with power. The power described is *dunamis,* and it means, "to have incredible, explosive, dynamic power." The military uniform we are to wear puts us in a position of winning. That makes it a good fight. We are equipped to beat the living daylights out of any foe that would dare assault us.

This uniform comes to us from fellowship with the Holy Spirit. This armor is God's, and He bestows it upon us as we fellowship with the Holy Spirit. We put on this new uniform by deliberately choosing to fellowship with the Holy Spirit. We all know that every man looks good in a uniform. When we put on our uniform—the armor of God—through fellowship with the Holy Spirit, we are empowered for winning a good fight.

Winning Personal Battles

During Jesus' days on earth, the Roman army was the world power. They were so committed to warfare that they practiced for it constantly. In their daily sword practice, the soldiers wielded shields that were made of heavy wood and were two times heavier than the ones used in actual battle. Every soldier practiced striking a death blow to the enemy using a wooden post fixed in the ground. The soldier was trained to take advantage of his enemy at his weakest point and learned how to strike him so he could not respond.

Flavius Vegetius Renatus, a high ranking officer with extensive knowledge of soldiers, penned the most influential military thesis ever known about Roman soldiers. He wrote that the soldiers were taught not to cut, but rather to thrust with their swords. The Romans not only made jest of those who fought with the edge of the weapon but always found them an easy conquest. A long stroke with the edge of the sword seldom kills since the vital parts of the body are defended both by the bones and armor. On the contrary, a stab, although it penetrates but two inches, can be fatal.

This knowledge of military training is what prompted

Paul to write about taking the sword of the Spirit, which is the Word of God (Ephesians 6:17). Using the sword of the Spirit is when a man who is in fellowship with the Holy Spirit speaks the Word of God and stabs the enemy a fatal blow with the Word.

When the Holy Spirit gives you a *rhema*, a word of God placed deep in your heart, you have sword power! It may only stab two inches deep, but it is powerful enough to annihilate your enemy. Your enemy is never flesh and blood. Your enemy is always the evil influence originating from hell, and the Word of God always triumphs over it.

The best example is when Jesus used the sword of the Spirit in Luke 4. Satan aggressively attacked Jesus several times. Jesus stabbed the enemy repeatedly with the Word of God by simply saying, "It is written...." The end result was that Jesus won the battle, and Satan retreated.

When a combat man is properly skilled with the sword of the Spirit (remember this comes through fellowship with the Holy Spirit), no battle is a real threat to him. Battles will become opportunities to prove your manhood.

Top Secret Information

We learned in earlier chapters that the Holy Spirit knows the seasons and times of our testing and rewards. He knows when the enemy is coming, which is another reason fellowship with the Holy Spirit is so wonderful. The Holy Spirit has access to the enemy's top secret information so the enemy will never catch us by surprise. We will be expecting him with our sword in our hand to greet him.

In 2 Chronicles 20, Jehoshaphat was told that the enemy was coming. The first thing he did was face his fear. He knew how to take courage from God by seeking direction from Him. We should always run to God when we have trouble. Fellowship with the Holy Spirit is the key to all victorious, fulfilled living.

Jehoshaphat began his fellowship with the Lord by focusing on the might and power of the Lord. This is the best way to begin! After we have praised and worshiped the Lord, then we can present our petitions to Him. After Jehoshaphat worshiped the Lord, he shared his problems and declared his complete dependence on God.

When we Man UP, it is okay to admit that we do not have the power to overcome the enemy on our own. Like Jehoshaphat, we can admit that we don't have a clue what to do and are completely dependent on the Holy Spirit. After I come into God's presence by praising and worshiping Him, I confess my fears and inability to overcome the enemy and admit my complete dependence on the Holy Spirit.

As a combat man, when I take my position in praise and worship of my great and powerful and awesome God, a fresh awareness of the Holy Spirit and His peace comes upon me. While I maintain a position/attitude of worship, the Lord goes to battle for me (2 Chronicles 20:16-17). When I put on my uniform and maintain my position of worship, I am prepared for battle (Ephesians 6:13-14). The Holy Spirit will bring the victory. This is a good fight! God is with me. What do I have to fear? I am more than a conqueror through Christ who saved me! I am a combat man. I am dressed for the battle. I have on my uniform. I have instructions from my commander (a rhema word). The sword of the Spirit is in my heart and hand. The battle is the Lord's, and He gives me victory. This is a good fight!

The world needs a few good men. Man UP and put on your uniform, the armor of God. You are more than a conqueror. Your kingdom (personal domain) will be defended and protected because you are the combat man!

Chapter 11

The Principled Man

Are you enjoying your role as the leading man in the movie of your life? Have you found the script fascinating thus far? What scenes have you enjoyed the most—the rain man, the fireman, or was it Superman? Which scene do you find yourself portraying today? According to the Internet, the following is a true story. It would make a great scene in a movie. Imagine if the following had happened to you.

On a weekend trip to Atlantic City, a woman won a bucketful of quarters at a slot machine. She took a break from the slots to have dinner with her husband in the hotel dining room. But first she wanted to stash the quarters in her room. "I'll be right back, and we'll go to eat," she told her husband and carried the coin-laden bucket to the elevator.

As she was about to walk into the elevator, she noticed two men already aboard. Both were black. One of them was tall . . . very tall . . . an intimidating figure. The woman froze. Her first thought was, *These two are going to rob me.* Her next thought was, *Don't be a bigot; they look like perfectly nice gentlemen.* But racial stereotypes are powerful, and fear immobilized her. She stood and stared at the two men. She felt anxious, flustered, and ashamed. She hoped they didn't read her mind but surely, they had to know what she was thinking!

Her hesitation about joining them in the elevator was all too obvious now. Her face was flushed. She couldn't just stand there, so with a mighty effort of will she picked up one foot and stepped forward and followed with the other foot and was on the elevator. Avoiding eye contact, she turned around stiffly and faced the elevator doors as they closed. A second passed, and then another second, and then another. Her fear increased! The elevator didn't move. Panic consumed her. *My God,* she thought, *I'm trapped and about to be robbed!* Her heart plummeted. Perspiration oozed from every pore.

Then one of the men said, "Hit the floor." Instinct told her to do what they told her. The bucket of quarters flew upwards as she threw out her arms and collapsed on the elevator floor. A shower of coins rained down on her. *Take my money and spare me,* she thought. More seconds passed. She heard one of the men say politely, "Ma'am, if you'll just tell us what floor you're going to, we'll push the button."

The one who said it had a little trouble getting the words out. He was trying mightily to hold in a belly laugh. The woman lifted her head and looked up at the two men. They reached down to help her up. Confused, she struggled to her feet. "When I told my friend here to hit the floor," said the average sized one, "I meant that he should hit the elevator button for our floor. I didn't mean for you to hit the floor, ma'am." He spoke genially. He bit his lip. It was obvious he was having a hard time not laughing. The woman thought,

My God, what a spectacle I've made of myself. She was too humiliated to speak. She wanted to blurt out an apology, but words failed her. How do you apologize to two perfectly respectable gentlemen for behaving as though they were going to rob you? She didn't know what to say.

The three of them gathered up the strewn quarters and refilled her bucket. When the elevator arrived at her floor, they insisted on walking her to her room. She seemed a little unsteady on her feet, and they were afraid she might not make it down the corridor. At her door, they bid her a good evening. As she sheepishly slipped into her room, she could hear them roaring with laughter all the way down the hall to the elevator.

The woman brushed herself off. She pulled herself together and went downstairs for dinner with her husband. The next morning, flowers were delivered to her room—a dozen roses. Attached to EACH rose was a crisp one hundred dollar bill. The card said, "Thanks for the best laugh we've had in years." It was signed: Eddie Murphy and Michael Jordan.

Life is full of funny situations and sometimes embarrassing situations as we learn to Man UP and respond properly to circumstances that confront us. We are a work in progress. We are learning to Man UP and live as men of God with the ability to choose the right course of action every time (Proverbs 2:6-9 NLT). However, we are learning, and sometimes we will make silly mistakes.

The Straw Watch

One day a man invented a priceless watch. This one-of-a-kind watch took the man his entire life to create. He meticulously fashioned a flawless watch that was made entirely of straw. To celebrate this invention, a huge reception was planned at an estate in the middle of the jungles of South America.

All the dignitaries and statesmen from around the world attended this open air reception. The watch was put on a glass pedestal so everyone could walk by and admire it as they passed through the reception line. Dinner was served, and the timepiece was left on display.

While everyone was engrossed in dinner and conversation, a donkey came wandering in out of the jungle and began to admire the straw watch. All of a sudden, the donkey opened his mouth and took a bite of it! Screams of horror and shock went through the crowd as they witnessed the donkey eating the watch. The moral to the story is that one jackass stunt can destroy a whole lifetime of work.

Some mistakes may be relatively harmless. Others may cost us everything. That is why we need the Holy Spirit as our comforter and guide. God never ends on a negative. He is the God of second chances and more. God is for us not against us (Psalm 56:9). If you are learning, you are not losing. You are being conformed to the image of Christ. To Man UP is to choose to live by the principles of Jesus Christ as the Holy Spirit conforms us to His image of true manhood.

Don't forget what we discussed in chapter nine. We learned there is a difference that needs to be understood between the person Jesus Christ and the principles of Jesus Christ. Jesus Christ the person was born of the virgin, lived a sinless life, was crucified for our sins, raised from the dead, has ascended to the right hand of the Father, and is coming again. Jesus is the way, the truth, and the life; and no man comes to the Father except by Him. Faith in what Jesus Christ did for us by grace causes us to be born again and inherit eternal life.

Many people know about the person Jesus Christ and have put their faith in His finished work. However, even if they were bald before they accepted Jesus Christ as their Savior, they were probably still bald after they accepted Jesus Christ. Nothing changed in the physical arena simply because they accepted Christ. Yes, indeed their sins were forgiven, and they are on their way to heaven. However, they need knowledge of the principles of Christ in order to make any changes in their lives.

This is why the Holy Spirit is so precious. We are God's workmanship. He is at work in us producing His fruit. Scripture says we are destroyed because of a lack of knowledge even though we have no lack of power or resources. It is the knowledge that we lack that produces our destruction (Hosea 4:6).

"In the beginning was the Word, and the Word was with God, and the Word was God" (John 1:1). In this verse if we substitute the word **word** with the word **principles**, we will be able to better understand the difference between the person of Jesus Christ and the principles of Jesus Christ. In the beginning were the Principles and the Principles were with God, and the Principles were God. And the Principles of God became flesh and dwelt among us, and we beheld His glory, the glory as of the only begotten of the Father, full of grace and truth.

Jesus took on the principles of God and physically lived them. As a result of His principled lifestyle, we were able to behold the glory of God in humanity. Jesus knew how to Man UP and showed us what a man living by the principles of God could accomplish. True peace, the lifestyle of God, the abundant life, and joy in living come when we know and accept the person Jesus Christ, and learn to Man UP and live by the principles of Jesus Christ.

Choices and Consequences

Every deed that was described in Scripture wasn't always the right thing to do. Scripture shows us the choices man made and the consequences of those choices. Moses shouldn't have killed his Egyptian brother. David should not have had Uriah killed. Paul should not have allowed strife to separate him from Barnabas. However, the Scriptures let us see that we are a people with the power of choice. We always reap the consequences of our choices.

Let's take a look at history for some examples of choices and consequences that man has encountered. How would you respond in each situation? It is 150 AD, and you live in the city of Rome. Roman civil law says that the father is the supreme ruler in his family. He has the legal right to abandon unwanted infants that are born in his household. The common practice is for these infants to be left outside the gates of the city. Christians are picking up these abandoned babies and taking them home to raise as their own children. The Roman civil authorities have declared this practice illegal. You are walking home and find one of these babies. Should you obey the civil law and ignore the child, or should you break the law by taking the child home?

Let's move ahead to 298 AD. The persecution of the

church is in full force. The civil authorities are rounding up all copies of the Scriptures from Christian churches. You are the pastor of a church. The authorities learn of this, and they arrive at your home, demanding that you turn over any and all copies that you have. You have several hidden in your home. They ask you if you own any. What would you do?

Move forward to 1941 AD. You are a Christian living in German-occupied Holland. You have been approached by a Jewish family seeking refuge from the Nazis. It is illegal to hide Jews, but they plead with you to hide them. Should you tell them to look for refuge elsewhere since you don't want to break the law?

Now it's 1955 AD. You live in Montgomery, Alabama. You are a black woman coming home from a hard day's work. You are sitting on a bus in the front section, which is legal as long as no white person is required to sit next to you. The bus fills up, and a white man is standing at the front of the bus. The bus driver tells you to get up and move to the back of the bus because a white person needs your seat. By law you are required to get up and let him sit there. You have paid your fare and local taxes to support the bus line. Should you stand up and move to the back of the bus?

You are a black person living in Alabama. You learn that Rosa Parks was arrested for refusing to give up her seat to stand in the back of the bus. The black community is organizing a boycott until the seating rule is abolished. The local ministers are supporting the boycott, and it seems to be working. The civil authorities discover a law that makes it illegal to run a boycott against any state or municipal service. Should you join the boycott?

You own an automobile at this time. Many in the black

community are seeking alternative ways to get to work and back home each day. You are asked by one of the boycott representatives to drive people to work and back home. The city has said this is illegal since there is a city ordinance requiring a minimum fee for all taxi services, and you will be regarded as a taxi service. Should you agree to drive people anyway?

Life requires that we Man UP and make choices. Choosing to live by the principles of Jesus Christ will produce righteous results. I would like to share four strategies that were used in Scripture when civil authorities went against the principles of Jesus Christ. They may surprise you. I trust they will help you Man UP with wisdom and tolerance without compromising the principles of Jesus Christ.

Strategies Used in Scripture

1. An individual knew that a law was wrong, and he protested verbally to the civil authority. **He obeyed the law, but he warned the civil authorities that the law was ungodly**. This is what Joab did when David insisted that the people should be numbered in a military census even though no battle was scheduled. Joab approached David and told him it was wrong and ungodly. Although he obeyed David's command, he did so under protest, reiterating that it was ungodly. Then God, in His righteous judgment, allowed a plague on Israel that killed seventy thousand people for David's unrighteous choice.

It has never been man's place to make somebody serve God. Vengeance is God's, not man's. It wasn't Joab's place to make David obey God. It was Joab's place to be a witness, a standard, a testimony, and a demonstration of what God wanted done. But it wasn't his responsibility to make somebody else bow the knee.

It is never our place to murmur either. Scripture clearly teaches that murmuring brings the curse on the one who murmurs. Praising God for who He is and being a demonstration of His standard bring about positive results in time. We are commanded to pray for our governmental authorities (1 Timothy 2:1-3). While we pray for those in authority, we should be praising God that they will bow the knee to righteousness, peace, and joy. We should not be murmuring about them to others or ourselves. God's Word doesn't return to Him void, so pray the Word over your government.

2. The protestor rebels against civil authority, warning the civil authority of the evil he is doing, and then the **protestor leaves the jurisdiction of that government**. Elijah did this when he told Jezebel and Ahab that it wouldn't rain for three years because of their unrighteousness. Then he hid in a cave to avoid the punishment of disobeying Ahab and Jezebel. I suggest you check out the cave scene before you use this strategy.

3. You **disobey the civil law that is unholy, and then you lie (use deception) to avoid punishment**. By the way, you risk death if you choose this strategy. I don't know that I completely understand the use of deception. I do know that when it was used by people in Scripture, it was used to keep a higher law of God (such as the preservation of life).

In Exodus the midwives in Moses' day were told to kill all male babies at birth. They refused to do so and then lied about it to avoid punishment.

But the midwives feared God, and did not do as the king of Egypt commanded them, but saved the male children alive. So the king of Egypt called for the midwives and said to them, Why have you done this thing, and saved the male children alive?' And the midwives said to Pharaoh, Because the Hebrew women are not like the Egyptian women; for they are lively and give birth before the midwives come to them.' Therefore God dealt well with the midwives, and the people multiplied and grew very mighty. And so it was because the midwives feared God that he provided households for them (Exodus 1:17-21).

How about military spying? Is that biblical and ethical? Can America send spies into other countries? Moses did. Joshua was one of the spies he sent into Canaan. About twenty years later, Joshua was the new commander-in-chief, and he sent spies into Jericho. To prevent them from being caught, a prostitute hid them and lied to the authorities about it.

So the king of Jericho sent to Rahab, saying, bring out the men who have come to you, who have entered your house, for they have come to search out all the country. Then the woman took the two men and hid them and she said, yes, the men came to me, but I did not know where they were from. And it happened as the gate was being shut when it was dark, but the men went out; where the men went I do not know, pursue them quickly, for you may find them (Joshua 2:3-5).

The prostitute hid them and then lied to avoid being caught. God blessed her and spared her and her entire household.

In these stated instances of using deception, one fact stands out to me. No one used deception on a covenant brother (fellow believer). Deception was only used against outright enemies of God. These principles also tells me that I may not always know what God is doing so I should be careful in my judgment and response to others. Let me share a personal story that vividly demonstrates this.

One day, I decided to Man UP and take my family to the beach. That sounds like a simple enough proposition, especially on a weekday. Wrong! This was during spring break, and the roads were jammed. I am not the most patient driver, and the tension was mounting as we inched toward the beach. Finally, I decided to take a short cut and head for the ferry, then take the ferry to the beach on the other side.

Bad move! Having come to the end of an alley, I saw that the line for the ferry extended way back. In time, I managed to join the end of the line. Right in front of me was a beer truck trying to back out of an alley. In order to help him, albeit with teeth clenched, I backed right back into the alley I had just left. He then signaled to me; that very alley was where he wanted to go. I then pulled out of the alley straight across the street into the next alley, to turn around and come back. Oops! The alley was posted, "No left turn." By this time, nothing was going to stop me. I had waited my turn to get in line already, and to drive around would delay me more than I was willing to be delayed. So I went ahead and made the left turn onto the street I had left to accommodate the beer truck. This left turn back into the line put me in back of the car I had been in front of before. This result was acceptable to me.

Two cars in back of me, a little old lady started screeching about line cutters and illegal left turns. I ignored her, so she got out of her car and came up to me, still carrying on about how I couldn't do that. I tried to explain, but she wasn't going to listen. She stomped off to get the security guard (a large, muscular fellow) who came over to question me. I explained to him what happened with the beer truck and all, but he just looked at me with "Yeah, sure" written on his face. He proceeded to ask the other cars if what I said was true, and they confirmed my tale. So he reassured the lady that everything was fine, but she really wasn't mollified.

You see, in her mind, she was absolutely right. Based on what she saw, I was a dirty line-cutting dog. She didn't know the whole situation and condemned me for what she thought she knew. This illustrates why I believe the next strategy is usually the most powerful choice.

4. The final strategy is **intercessory prayer for those in authority**. Prayer is powerful.

> *If my people who are called by my name will humble themselves, and pray and seek my face, and turn from their wicked ways, then I will hear from heaven, and will forgive their sin and heal their land* (2 Chronicles 7:14).

Daniel used the strategy of prayer. It brought results that changed an entire nation. Prayer has not lost its power! As you have read this book, you have seen that the secret to manhood is intimacy with the Holy Spirit. He gives us the wisdom and the power for manhood. The Holy Spirit helps us pray when we don't know how to pray.

Romans 8 is about the Holy Spirit praying through us in order that the whole of creation can be delivered from corruption. Whatever the issue we may be facing, whatever strategy we may need, we can pray in the spirit and receive the wisdom of God. Praise the Lord. What a wonderful gift!

We discovered in chapter two that courage is knowledge God is with us wherever we go (Joshua 1:9). This knowledge comes from spending time with Him in fellowship. As we fellowship with God, our joy and our wisdom increases. Let's partner with God and cherish His authority in our lives. God is always smarter than we are. We can receive His wisdom when we pray in the Spirit. We are champions through Him. *"Through God we will do courageously, for it is He who shall tread down our enemies!"* (Psalm 108:13).

A New Man

When you make the decision to Man UP and live by the principles of Scripture, you will discover that life is never boring. You will be transformed into a new breed of man. You will have accomplished the manhood mandate. Saul is an example of a man who was changed and given the ability to Man UP. Something amazing happened *"Then the Spirit of the Lord will come upon you, and you will . . . be turned into another man"* (1 Samuel 10:6).

Scripture says that the Holy Spirit came upon Saul, He gave him a new heart, and Saul became a new man! You can become a new man. You can choose to accept Jesus Christ as your personal Savior and pursue His principles for living. The Holy Spirit will become your best friend, and you will accomplish great feats through partnership with Him. I believe that the Spirit of the Lord has been coming upon you just as He came upon Saul, as you have been reading this book. I believe you will from this day forward have the ability to Man UP. You are becoming a new man!

The Champion Pursuit

One evening on the way home from a wonderful dinner and time of fellowship in the home of our friends Pat and Shirley Boone, I expressed to Darlene that I wished I could sing like Pat Boone. It would be wonderful to have such a gift and bring joy to so many people. (Pat is one of the top all-time record sellers.) Darlene then asked me, "Why don't you take voice lessons?" Boom! It hit me like a rock. I really didn't want to sing like Pat Boone, or I would have taken voice lessons.

The proof of our desire is our pursuit! What are you pursuing? Do you truly desire to Man UP and live by the principles of Jesus Christ? True manhood can only be experienced when we pursue intimacy with the Holy Spirit. As men, this is the most courageous and wise thing we could ever do.

The fact that you are reading this book is evidence of your desire to Man UP and become a champion for Christ. The champion is in you (1 John 4:4), waiting to be released. The future is yours for the taking. Whatever mistakes we have made, whatever needs to be fixed, we can trust the Holy Spirit and make the right choices beginning today. Your past does not determine your future when you Man UP and cultivate intimacy with the Holy Spirit. The Holy Spirit will teach you the principles of Jesus Christ, and you will choose the right course of action every time.

My child, listen to me and treasure my instructions. Tune your ears to wisdom, and concentrate on understanding. Cry out for insight and understanding. Search for them as you would fir lost money or hidden treasure. Then you will understand what it means to fear the Lord, and you will gain knowledge of God. For the Lord grants wisdom! From his mouth come knowledge and understanding. He grants a treasure of good sense to the godly. He is their shield, protecting those who walk with integrity. He guards the paths of justice and protects those who are faithful to him. Then you will understand what is right, just, and fair, and you will know how to find the right course of action every time" (Proverbs 2:1-9 NLT).

Here is a simple prayer to settle forever that you are a new man. Pray this prayer out loud and begin your new journey.

Heavenly Father, I choose to accept Jesus Christ as my Savior. I choose to turn away from living life without Your power. I want to Man UP and become all You have created me to be. Give me a new heart like You did for Saul. Thank you for the gift of your Holy Spirit who will never leave me or forsake me. In Jesus' name, amen!

My friend, you have begun the champion's journey of manhood. The champion in you will emerge and always be triumphant.

Chapter 12

The Fixed Man

I am aware that a chapter entitled "The Fixed Man" in a book entitled *Man UP* probably elicits some snickers from the readers. Many men have endured being "fixed" from the ability to impregnate a woman by having a vasectomy. That procedure is usually not laughed at until it is over and we have survived. When things need to be fixed, the healing process can be painful. Whatever may need to be fixed in our lives will require that we Man UP and endure the process.

Have you ever tried to fix something major or beyond your ability to fix? I'll never forget the time I had to fix a U-Haul truck that I had rented. Money was tight at that time. Our family was moving into a different neighborhood. When I rented the U-Haul truck, they offered me the option of purchasing insurance to cover any damage to the vehicle while I had it rented. I did not want to spend the extra fifteen dollars, so I declined the coverage.

It was lightly raining while we loaded the truck with our possessions and moved to the new neighborhood. When we had finished unloading the truck, it was too late in the evening to return the U-Haul to the rental yard. I parked the

152

truck in the street in the front of our new home and decided to return it the next morning. I thanked the men from the church who had helped me move and went to bed.

When I got up early the next morning, it was still drizzling outside. I examined the U-Haul, and to my horror, the left rear quarter panel was dented and hanging by three very loose rivets. I panicked! I cried. I had outbursts of something other than a spiritual language. I just knew U-Haul would charge me thousands of dollars for this damage. Why hadn't I taken the insurance coverage?

I called Ron, one of the church elders, who was a good fix-it man. I took the truck to his house and pulled the damaged quarter panel off it (with one little tug). I went to Home Depot and purchased a rivet gun and rivets. The rivet gun cost me more than the insurance coverage would have cost.

Ron and I laid the quarter panel on blocks of wood and with rubber hammers attempted to straighten out the concave piece of metal. We even laid plywood over it and drove over the plywood, hoping that would do the trick. We made some improvement, but you could definitely see that it was damaged. We riveted the panel back onto the truck. We were a comic sight in the drizzling rain.

With our repair attempt complete, I drove the truck back to the rental yard. All the way back, I was praying and pleading with God to please not let U-Haul see the damage and take the truck back as if everything was okay.

"Praise the Lord!" I cried out as I left U-Haul. They had received the truck back as is, did not charge me any extra, and I was free.

The next day was Sunday. Before I shared the morning

message, I thanked the men for helping me move and shared with the church the story of the repair. While I was telling the story of fixing the damaged truck, the men who helped me move began laughing out loud. Their great belly laughter was so loud I had to stop and ask the men what was so funny. They said, "Pastor, you don't understand. That truck was in that broken condition when you picked it up at U-Haul!"

Embarrassed, humiliated, foolish . . . I felt it all at that moment. At least U-Haul benefited from my attempts to fix the truck.

The word *fixed* has many meanings. One of the meanings is, "to repair or restore to wholeness." We learned in an earlier chapter that we are called to be repairmen. Let's focus for a moment on the truth that the Holy Spirit desires to fix us as men. Remember Christlikeness and manhood are synonymous. The Holy Spirit will fix whatever is lacking in our being that needs to be conformed to the image of Christ.

The Holy Spirit has been working in you as you have been reading this book. As a consequence, there may have been some areas of your manhood that have been fixed and restored to the wholeness God intends for you.

A Predetermined Outcome

Another meaning for fixed is a predetermined outcome. Some people think that great sporting events such as championship boxing or the Super Bowl are fixed. It is suspected that sinister forces have rigged the game for gambling purposes and predetermined the outcome of the game. While I think the possibility of fixing these games is remote, history has proven that it has happened on occasion.

God has a predetermined outcome scheduled for your life (Jeremiah 29:11). He desires for you to Man UP and become a champion for Christ.

> *Blessed is the man who fears the Lord, Who delights greatly in His commandments. His descendants will be mighty on earth; the generation of the upright will be blessed. Wealth and riches will be in his house, and his righteousness endures forever. Unto the upright there arises light in the darkness; He is gracious, and full of compassion, and righteous. A good man deals graciously and lends; He will guide his affairs with discretion. Surely he will never be shaken; the righteous will be in ever-lasting remembrance. He will not be afraid of evil tidings; His heart is fixed, trusting in the Lord* (Psalm 112:1-7).

God has fixed it so that when we Man UP, we will be blessed men. Our children and grandchildren will be mighty on earth. They will be people who have significant influence. God has fixed it so that when you Man UP, you will bring light into the darkness by having revelation knowledge. You will have the wisdom of what to do when confusion surrounds others. God has fixed it so that when you Man UP, you will have wealth and riches in your home. You will have the ability to lend and not be forced to borrow. God has fixed it so that when you Man UP, you will guide your affairs with discretion. You will be a wise and discreet businessman who will not be shaken when bad news is announced. These fixed results have been predetermined by God for the man **who has a fixed heart.**

A Fixed Heart

What is a fixed heart? Fixed can also be defined as being focused or single-minded. When your heart is fixed, you are focused on the Holy Spirit and the fact that He is with you. This is what David calls a fixed or steadfast heart. David had become so fixed in his heart that God was with him, he was able to confidently say, *"I am not afraid, for I know my enemies will flee because God is for me"* (Psalm 56:3-11).

David knew that God's predetermined outcome for his life would become a reality. He knew that the Holy Spirit was fixing everything that was necessary for his God-given destiny to become manifested in his life. David had determined from his youth to be fixed on the truth that God was for him.

Men, **God is for you and not against you.** Get fixed on this truth. The Holy Spirit is fixing all that is necessary to ensure that God's predetermined outcome will be a reality in your life.

It is interesting to note that science has discovered the heart is formed before the brain in the womb. So too do we need our hearts fixed on the Holy Spirit, and then our minds will be renewed to God's predetermined outcome for our life.

Dr. Pearsall gave a lecture on the heart, and a psychiatrist in the audience told the story of one of her patients. An eight-year-old girl was the recipient of a heart transplant from a ten-year-old girl who had been raped and murdered.

The 8-year-old began to have nightmares after she received the heart from the 10-year-old victim. The psychiatrist decided to tell the police about the dreams the girl was having. The dreams were about the rape and murder that the 10-year-old donor had experienced.

Based on what the 8-year-old told the police, they arrested the neighbor of the 10-year-old who had been killed. The 8-year-old had described in such detail what the house looked like where the murder occurred and what the conversation was between the victim and the murderer, that the neighbor was convicted of the murder.

The heart knew it. The brain and the body of the donor were gone, but the heart knew it. Scripture says we must guard our hearts carefully because it is from our heart that all the issues of life spring forth (Matthew 15:19; Proverbs 4:23).

It is all a matter of heart. Fix your heart on the truth that you are choosing to Man UP and become a champion for Christ. Get your heart fixed on the truth that the Holy Spirit is with you. He is fixing whatever needs to be fixed in your life. Submit to His workmanship. Get your heart fixed on the truth that God is for you and not against you. God wants you to be all you can be.

How does my heart get fixed? It gets fixed as I read the Scriptures and focus on the truths I discover in the Bible. My heart gets fixed as I pray and praise and worship my heavenly Father. God said if we will ask Him, He will give us a new heart with the right desires (Ezekiel 36:26). Man UP and ask God for your new heart and keep it fixed on Him.

A Man UP Dinner

In Luke 24:13-32, the story is told of Jesus walking with some disciples on the road to Emmaus. The disciples did not recognize that it was Jesus walking and talking with them. He seemed to simply be a stranger discussing the current events of the past weekend with them as they walked the seven mile trip to Emmaus.

The death, burial, and resurrection of Jesus Christ had just taken place. This group of disciples (not the original twelve but a group associated with them) was emotionally distraught over the events. They had lost their leader and their hope for the future. The women in their group had been to the tomb and reported to these men that it was empty and possibly there had been a resurrection. The men likely dismissed the women's viewpoint as a result of emotional trauma and were discussing this conclusion when the resurrected Jesus walked up to them.

They did not know it was Him. Somehow they were prevented from recognizing the resurrected Jesus. He began by asking them what caused them to be so sad. They responded, "Are you the only stranger in Jerusalem who doesn't know what has happened this past weekend?" Thus began an intense conversation about Jesus and all that had happened.

Jesus said to them, "You are such foolish people and slow of heart to believe." Then He began with Moses and expounded to them the Scriptures concerning Himself. As they drew closer to home, the men invited Jesus, still unrecognized, to stay and have dinner with them. Jesus accepted their invitation.

Before they began to eat, Jesus gave the blessing, and their eyes were suddenly opened. They knew it was Jesus, and instantly He vanished from their sight! Wow. What a time! They were instantly able to Man UP and recognize Jesus.

The men said to one another, "Didn't our hearts burn within us while He talked with us and opened the Scriptures to us?" Jesus had performed heart surgery on them, and they were unaware what was going on until it was finished!

As you have been reading *Man UP*, some of it may have sounded strange to you at first. You may now be realizing that your heart has been strangely warmed as you were reading. Jesus, through His Holy Spirit, has been fixing your heart. The Scriptures coming alive to you have settled some issues and enabled you to Man UP.

You will have many characters to play as you perform the leading man role in the movie of your life. Some of the roles you will perform will be more delightful than others. All of them will demand courage as you make tough decisions. If you have decided to Man UP, you will discover the right course of action to take in every situation.

You are being fixed as a man, learning how to focus on the Holy Spirit who is with you. The Holy Spirit is fixing all that concerns you. God's predetermined blessings will become a reality in your life.

Begin to thank God and praise Him right now. Experience the greatness God has for you as you Man UP!

About the Author

Dr. Cliff Self served in the U.S. Air Force and then continued his education while serving as a youth pastor. After ordination he served as senior pastor in a major denominational church. Dr. Cliff founded Courageous Living Christian Center and served there as senior pastor for twenty years. Afterwards he returned to school to complete his doctorate and became a professor of biblical studies at Bethel Christian College.

While still a young pastor, Dr. Cliff was privileged to travel with Dr. Ed Cole for many of his Maximized Manhood campaigns. He has appeared on many radio and television programs and written four books. Dr. Cliff is an inspirational speaker known for his humor and practical application of biblical wisdom.

He has been married to his wife, Darlene, for 37 years, and they have two children and three grandchildren. They reside in southern California.

Dr. Cliff may be contacted at Courageous Living Ministries, PO Box 53810, Irvine, CA 92619 or you can visit his website: www.courageouslm.com.